FIRST EASTER

Books by Catherine Marshall

Prepared from Peter Marshall's Sermons

THE FIRST EASTER

PETER MARSHALL

Chosen Books
A Division of Baker Book House
Grand Rapids, Michigan 49516

Published by Chosen Books
a division of Baker Book House Company
P.O. Box 6287, Grand Rapids, MI 49516-6287

Printed in the United States of America

Library of Congress Cataloging-in-Publication Data

Marshall, Peter, 1902–1949.
    [First Easter]
    Peter Marshall's the first Easter / edited and with an introduction by Catherine Marshall.
      p. cm.
    ISBN 0-8007-9120-7
    1. Easter—Sermons. 2. Jesus Christ—Resurrection—Sermons. 3. Sermons, American. 4. Presbyterian Church—Sermons. I. Marshall, Catherine, 1914–1983. II. Title. III. Title: First Easter.
BV4259.M34   1988
232.9′7—dc19   87-30876

Foreword

Once again we at Chosen Books are bringing out a new edition of Peter Marshall's *The First Easter*. There have been so many previous editions of this book published that I have lost count.

Why does *The First Easter* always seem fresh and new? What draws people back to this particular telling of the old, old story of Jesus' death and resurrection?

In thinking over these questions I went back to the year 1959, the original publication date of *The First Easter*. Catherine Marshall had been Peter's widow for over ten years when we were married in November of that year 1959. Soon after the wedding I was adapting one of Peter's sermons for a *Guideposts* magazine feature. My fascination with the man and his works began at that point and continues to this day.

Why is *The First Easter* so vivid? Because as the story unfolds Peter takes the reader by the hand and takes him/her back nearly 2,000 years to the happening itself. We see the men gathered in the Upper Room, sense their fear, hear the footsteps at midnight along cobbled streets, smell the dank graveclothes in the tomb. *We are there while the greatest story of all time is happening.*

The First Easter is timeless. Peter Marshall's rendition is unforgettable. That's why this book will be issued and reissued for many years to come. It's always new.

Leonard LeSourd

Introduction

How is it that the interest in Peter Marshall, Scottish immigrant-pastor and chaplain of the United States Senate in the late 1940s, lives on so long after his death?

Surely, it must be because our basic human needs are much the same in any decade, no matter how the modern wrappings change. And because Peter Marshall's preaching and prayers gave answers to people—and still do. He knew that those answers would not come through any wisdom of his, but only as he introduced people, all kinds of people—Mr. Jones or Mrs. Smith—to the living Lord who always has the solution we seek.

One reason that Peter had an extraordinary ability to introduce ordinary folks, including the young, to "the Chief," as he liked to call his Lord, was that the preacher himself had been led into the ministry out of a working-class background. This included a machinist's job in Scottish iron-and-tube works, then emigration to America, and to Columbia Theological Seminary by way of digging ditches in New Jersey and newspaper work in Alabama.

Thus from the beginning this Scot with the burr to his r's was more concerned with reaching those who had no notion about Christianity then he was with appealing to settled church members.

Passion and burning conviction poured out of the preacher's own experience as he revealed how much a contemporary Lord wants to rescue us, guide our lives, heal hurting bodies, mend marriages and homes in trouble, comfort the sorrowing, challenge each one of us to rise above mediocre living, restore the joy of living to jaded, disillusioned hearts.

To Peter Marshall, the compass needle of Christianity pointed inevitably to Resurrection morning. He lavished his best thinking, his most careful preparation, and all his gifts for sermonizing through the years on his Easter messages. In these messages, his ability to paint a picture in words, to enable his listeners to see and hear and feel an incident, rose to its greatest height.

After Peter's death I found in my possession 96 Easter manuscripts from eighteen years and four months of preaching. In reviewing these sermons covering the events of Passion Week, I quickly found myself caught up in drama—sheer, engrossing drama, at times tender, at times terrible. And always I found myself moved by Peter's ability to enlist the emotions on the side of faith.

Thus *The First Easter* unfolded itself. My only part in it was to shape from the many sermons Dr. Marshall's re-creation of each scene as event followed event, and to edit the material only where necessary to weave it together.

Here, then, is Easter—the triumphant morning of Christianity—seen through the eyes and described from the heart of one man.

Catherine Marshall

THE FIRST EASTER

What is this mysterious, strange, joyous influence that seems to permeate everything at this time of the year . . . that lingers, like a sweet perfume, delicate and clean, to touch us all with its magic?

It is an intriguing thing . . . intangible, yet real.

We feel it . . .
    sense it . . .
        thrill to it.

There is more to it than bunny rabbits
    and colored eggs
        and gay new clothes.

Easter is more than a celebration
    because the sap is rising in the trees . . .
        and the bare branches are slipping bright green rings
        on bony fingers . . .
    and blossoms are turning wood and garden into fairy-land.

Easter is more than a spring festival.
So far as the Church is concerned, the message of Easter is contained in the declaration
                "Christ is Risen!"

Did the Lord really rise from the dead?

Is it true that He is alive?
   Was that tomb in Jerusalem really empty?
      Can we believe it?
Do we believe it?

Either we are dealing here with flaming truth or the hideous
falsehood of the Christian Gospel.
It is important that we know which.

For if the Resurrection is a fact, then the events that took
place in the city of Jerusalem between the 14th Nisan and the
16th Nisan in the year 3790 or—as we now record time—
between April 7 and April 9, Anno Domini 30, are the most
important and significant events in history.

What did happen?

Hear that story as it is given us. . . .

It was night.

Outside in the streets of Jerusalem, shadows fled before a
full moon rising over the pinnacles of the Temple.
Time was ebbing toward its close—and its beginning—the
cleft that would for the rest of recorded history mark it
            Before Christ . . . After Christ. . . .

A sinister silence beat in upon the heavy hearts of a group of
twelve men gathered in an Upper Room.

They knew that something dreadful was about to happen
and they were apprehensive.
This was the last night of Jesus' life on earth.
He had looked forward to this occasion—
       having His own apostles—
     His chosen friends—
   His intimate companions
for three years grouped around Him in the fellowship of the
Last Supper.

He had Himself made the arrangements for the supper.
"Look for a man carrying a pitcher of water," He had told
His disciples.
That in itself would be an unusual thing
  for it was the women who usually carried the water.
The man would lead them to this Upper Room, perhaps in
the home of John Mark's father—a guest room built on the
flat roof of the house.

Pillars supported a roof closed in with curtains, and
the curtains billowed and swung in a cool evening breeze.
A lamp hanging from the ceiling cast flickering light.

The men were reclining on couches around a low
U-shaped table.
At the Master's left was Simon Peter . . . at His right, John.

A quiet voice spoke:
     "With desire I have desired to eat this Passover
     with you before I suffer. . . ."

Bronzed hands took a loaf of bread . . .
  gave thanks for it . . .
    broke it . . .

"This is My body which is given for you:
this do in remembrance of Me. . . ."

The Last Supper was to institute a memorial—the loving
desire to be remembered.

Christ relied upon homely symbols—
   a piece of bread,
      a cup of the juice of the lowly grape—
to recall Him to future generations.

He knew that we would be in constant danger of
forgetting Him . . .
Therefore He enlisted sense on the side of faith and trusted
to these simple everyday memorials for the recalling
to our treacherous memories of His undying love.

> "This is My blood of the new testament [a new
> agreement] which is shed for many for the
> remission of sins. . . . Drink ye all of it. . . .

> "But I say unto you, I will not drink henceforth of
> this fruit of the vine, until that day when I drink
> it new with you in My Father's Kingdom."

Strange words with which to institute a sacrament.
What did He mean?
The words that fell from His lips that night are standing
evidence of Christ's own estimate as to where the center of
His work lies—
   We are to remember His death.
Never did He ask that we should commemorate His
birth . . .

Not once did He request that any of the wonderful deeds
He performed should be immortalized . . .
Only this—His last and greatest work—
                    the work of redemption.

This was to be His memorial—a cross—to remind us that
God's love for us is a love
    that hate cannot nullify
        and death cannot kill.

Already, days before, He had told His apostles:
            "Behold, we go up to Jerusalem . . . the Son of Man
            . . . shall be mocked, and spitefully entreated . . .
            and they shall scourge Him, and put Him to death;
            and the third day He shall rise again. . . ."

Outside the night was silent, as if all Jerusalem held its
breath,
feeling the approach of the storm.
Like sequins, the lights of the city reappeared
                    twinkling one by one.

And an indigo sky grew darker and darker.
One by one the city's noises were silenced.
But in the room itself there was noise, for the disciples
were quarreling.

Their argument had started earlier in the day as they had
walked to the supper.

Then they had divided into smaller groups, so as not
to attract too much attention as they gathered for
the evening meal.

Because there were no servants to bathe their feet and
because they had been arguing about who was to be chief
among them, nobody had made any gesture of ceremonial
washing.

They had walked past the earthenware pitcher of water at
the door and had taken their places around the table—

angry

argumentative

sulking

cross

tired.

We can imagine them stretching out their robes so as to cover
their feet—trying to pretend there was nothing wrong—
when everything was wrong.
They had looked like sulky schoolboys.
Who wanted to stoop to do a slave's work?

Now, during the supper, Jesus rose and took off His outer
garment.

Then He took a towel, girded Himself, poured water into the
basin, and began to do the menial thing that not one of them
would do—
He began to wash the disciples' feet.

> And He did it because he was the Son of God.

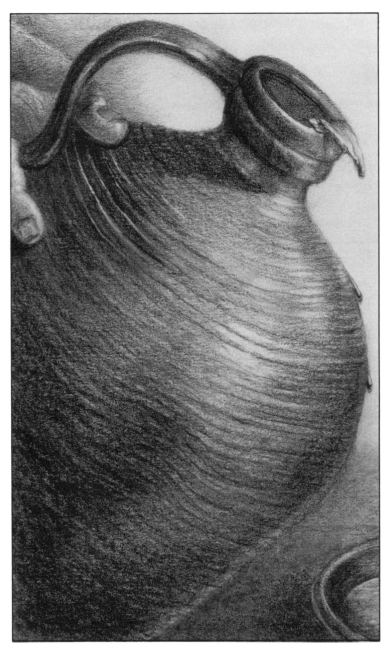

That lowly loving deed expressed in all its loneliness
the glory and humility of His own heart.

Did the apostle John tell us of this incident so that we might
understand that those who shared the Last Supper with
Jesus of Nazareth were no plaster saints?
These were ordinary men—quite like you and me—
   subject to nerves and temper
      to pettiness and self-centeredness.

John makes a very significant statement in telling of this
incident. He says:

> "Jesus knowing that the Father had given all things
> into His hands, and that He was come from God,
> and went to God; He riseth from supper . . . and
> began. . . ."

To reveal His death by signs and miracles? No.
To show His authority by displays of superhuman power?
No.
To act like an all-powerful dictator? No, no.

Christ, knowing who He was, having come forth from God,
knowing that He was going to God, began to "wash the
disciples' feet."

The glory of Christ's life on earth was not the ethereal glory
of the supernatural . . .

No—but rather the simple fact that He loved us,
   that He loved unlovely men and women

with a love that goes on loving—and goes on loving—so that nothing can ever defeat it . . .
Nothing can ever break it down.

"Having loved his own which were in the world," adds John,
"He loved them unto the end."

Then Christ again took His place at the table.

All eyes were upon Him.
And a look like shadows blotting out the sun crossed the Master's face.

> "Verily, I say unto you, that one of you shall betray Me. . . ."

The apostles were shocked.
Peter blurted out, "Lord, surely it isn't I?"
And one by one they all asked, "Lord, is it I?"

> "He it is, to whom I shall give a sop, when I have dipped it."

Judas was sitting second from the Master on the right, with John between them.
Jesus had known all along that Judas had been plotting.
He knew that Judas had gone to the chief priests some days before and had offered to help them arrest Him.
For Caiaphas, the high priest, had long since decided that this Jesus of Nazareth must be gotten out of the way.

So Christ took a piece of bread and, dipping it in a bowl of haroseth, handed it to Judas.

And slowly Judas rose to his feet.
He strode toward the stairway, then pausing
with one hand on the heavy curtains, he turned
and faced Christ.

An awful look passed between them—
  sorrow on the face of the Master . . .
    determination, strain, evil on the swarthy face of
    Judas.
Then he turned and was gone.
The curtains swung behind him.
There was silence.

And John adds, "And it was night. . . ."

T he eleven men who were left were very quiet.
The voice of Christ was very soft and low—
tender with farewell.
It was now only a matter of hours until Christ and His
disciples would be separated.
He wished to fill those last hours of fellowship with the
tenderest and most significant of His teachings.

The most sacred
  the most tender
    the most heartfelt emotions
are those expressed at the end of the letter. . . .

The tenderest caress comes just before the parting.
The softest word just before the conversation is ended
                              before the train pulls out
                              before we turn away.

We seem to catch the quiet intimacy of that fellowship.
Unforgettable words of parting and comfort were spoken by
Jesus to His friends.
John has written them out for us:

> "Little children . . . a new commandment I give
> unto you, That ye love one another; as I have loved
> you. . . . By this shall all men know that ye are
> My disciples. . . .

> "Let not your heart be troubled. . . . In My Father's
> house are many mansions: if it were not so, I would
> have told you. . . .

> "I will not leave you comfortless: I will come to
> you. . . .

> "I am the vine, ye are the branches. . . . Abide in
> Me, and I in you. . . .

> "These things I have spoken unto you, that in Me
> ye might have peace. In the world ye shall have
> tribulation: but be of good cheer; I have overcome
> the world. . . ."

Overcome the world? When the One who spoke was so soon
to fall under the power of Caesar?

Yes, for in reality we must remember that Jesus could have
escaped the cross.

No one compelled Him to go to Jerusalem on that last journey.
Indeed, His friends and apostles urged Him not to go.

Watch Him in the bitter hours that lie immediately ahead, time after time taking the initiative in deciding His own fate.

Christ had begun His ministry by telling His apostles that the Son of Man must suffer many things.
Must—there was no other way.
It was for that purpose that He had come into the world.

> "As Moses lifted up the serpent in the wilderness, even so must the Son of Man be lifted up; that whosoever believeth in Him should not perish, but have everlasting life."

There was Light in the little room that night.
But beyond the light lay a death-ridden world . . .
   in the midst of the military might that was Rome
        where life was cheap . . .
   in the philosophers' porticoes of Athens
        where the mind found no hope . . .
   in the dangerous living of the great shipping centers of Asia Minor to the disease-infested alleys of old Jerusalem—
Men feared death, dodged its hideous grasp, could nowhere find respite from their fear.

But here was something new. . . .
Here was One facing death—not afraid, but confident . . .
   already triumphant . . .
   already speaking about seeing His friends again . . .
   about never leaving them. . . .

Strange words . . . about being with them to the uttermost
parts of the earth and to the end of time.

How? Why? Because He alone knew the Father's eternal
purpose for what it was—the determination once and for all
to destroy the power of death—
once and for all to deliver men from their lifelong bondage to
the fear of death.

Within a matter of hours, Christ Himself was to become the
instrument by which the Father would—for all time—make
death not a wall . . . but a door.

T he Last Supper was over.
And when they had sung a hymn, they went out into the
dark and deserted streets.
It was almost midnight.
Past the Lower Pool and through the Fountain Gate
they walked slowly, moving in little silent clusters.
For a time the narrow cobblestone street, banked high in
the middle, led beside the brook Cedron.

The group moved up the hill
toward their favorite rendezvous—
                 a garden called Gethsemane.

Here in the deep shadows of the night, moving along in the
deeper shadows of the trees, they halted.

A few lights twinkled on the hill opposite, but most of the
city was asleep, for it was now after midnight.
They could see the Temple, its spire tipped with gold,
glistening in the moonlight.
And from the ramparts of the Fortress Antonia they could
hear a Roman sentry calling his watch.

As they stood there looking across the valley at the holy city,
they wondered at the strange turn events had taken.
They remembered the reechoing shouts of the people . . .
                           the glad Hosannas . . .
                    and the crown that had been refused.
Some of them were thinking of how Judas had left their
fellowship to move out into the darkness.
They were wondering where he was and what he was doing.

The eleven could not know that the betrayer had already
agreed to Caiaphas' offer of thirty pieces of silver—
     the cost of a slave, it was—
Or that Caiaphas was even then moving under cover of the
velvet night to seek audience with the Roman procurator . . .

          "If the Nazarene is captured this night, will you
          agree to sit in the Tribunal to condemn Him
          on the morrow?"

The group moved on into the garden under the gnarled
old trees.
The odor of the olive presses clung to the still night air.

And now there was a period of waiting, as though the
Master deliberately waited for some rendezvous with des-
tiny—
His apostles knew not what.

Once again He could easily have escaped; yet He did not.
There was plenty of time, so much time that the weary
apostles—propped against the olive trees—fell asleep.

While they slept, Christ prayed . . .
   kneeling under the little gray-green leaves that gleamed
   white where the moonlight filtered through.
Was there then no way, no other way? . . .
      "Father, all things are possible unto Thee; take away
      this cup from Me. . . ."
"This cup". . .
Often Christ had seen the bodies of the crucified hanging on
the hill outside the Gennath Gate. . . .
Sometimes He had heard their moans and their curses,
seen them writhing in their final agony.

Jesus of Nazareth was a man—a real man.
Every bit of His manhood shrank from such an end.

And Luke tells us:
      ". . . Being in an agony He prayed more earnestly:
      and His sweat was as it were great drops of blood
      falling down to the ground."

Already He was living the pain of it.
Could ultimate triumph come in no other way?

Human sin—man fleeing God—was capable of dreadful deeds.
Of course . . . but must He be the One to taste every depth that sin could devise . . .
      misunderstanding
    betrayal
  desertion by friends
expediency
weakness
 callousness
  deliberate cruelty
    excruciating pain
      death itself . . .
in order to prove finally and forever that no evil is any match for the Father?

The worn face glistening with sweat—so young in time—
  grown so old in understanding . . .
    bowed in final surrender. . . .

    "Nevertheless, not what I will, but what Thou wilt."

The stillness of the garden was suddenly broken by the low sound of voices. . . .
And now a flickering torch came into view . . .
              and another
              and another.
Surely this was a procession.
There were soldiers. . . .
Twigs crackled under their feet and they stooped low as they passed under the olive trees.
Someone in front carried a swinging lantern.

A nondescript mob it was—a rabble of indiscriminate
ruffians—the hangers-on of the Temple . . .
            soldiers
        Temple guards
      Temple doorkeepers
  little priests with big ambitions . . .
who had laid aside their rings of heavy keys . . .
exchanged their brooms for staves and spears and blud-
geons—armed to the teeth, determined to capture the most
peaceable One who ever walked upon the earth.

Out of that sickening crowd there stepped a familiar figure.
It was Judas, a smile upon his face.
"Hail, Master," he said . . . and kissed Him with a kiss that
must have burned Christ's cheek.

Thus identified, Christ was seized . . .
          bound with ropes . . .
        His hands manacled
      His arms tied to His side.

The disciples, too, were caught in the trap.
After a moment's hesitation, some of them seemed to gain
courage, to think of fighting in defense of their Master.

One asked, "Lord, shall we smite with the sword?"
And Peter—not waiting for the answer—drew from the folds
of his cloak a short sword . . .
      more like a dagger . . .
and recklessly struck a vicious blow at the nearest enemy.

It happened to be the high priest's servant, whose name was
Malchus—and the blow severed his right ear.

But when Christ saw what Peter had done, He quickly commanded him to put up his sword:

"They that take the sword shall perish with the sword."

The method of Peter was the sword . . .
The method of Christ was a cross . . .
Peter sought revenge . . .
Christ sought reconciliation.

Peter cried, "Give me a sword, and we can advance
the Kingdom."
Christ cried, "Give Me a cross, and I, if I be lifted up, will draw all men unto Me."

And so they led Him away as a butcher might drag a steer to the slaughterhouse.

Simon Peter had seen the last flickering torch disappear round the turn of the path that wound down the hill. . . . Only once in a while could the lights of the procession be seen through the trees—like giant fireflies.

The murmur of voices died away,
    the crackling of twigs
        and the rustling of dislodged stones through the grass.
There swept over Peter the realization that his Master had at last been captured and was marching away to die.

The icy fear that gripped his heart was a startling contrast to the flaming courage with which he had drawn his short sword a few minutes before, for this was a different Peter.

He realized that he had blundered, and that he had been
rebuked.
Disappointed and puzzled, he could not understand the
calm submission with which Christ had permitted them to
bind His hands and march Him off.

Realizing that he stood alone in the deserted garden, Peter
stumbled blindly down the trail, heedless of the twigs that
lashed his face and tore at his robes.

Stumbling on down the hill, instinctively hurrying to catch
up with the others, and yet not anxious to get too close, he
followed down to the foot of the Mount of Olives, across the
brook Cedron, and back up the hill to old Jerusalem, still
asleep and quiet.

The procession made first for the house of Annas, into which
they escorted Jesus.
The heavy door creaked shut behind Him, and when Peter
approached timidly, it was to find John standing there.

John persuaded the girl stationed at the door to let them in
and, as they slipped past her, she scrutinized Peter and said
to him:
    "Art not thou also one of this man's disciples?"
He said, "I am not."

Perhaps she felt that she could speak to Peter.
Perhaps she felt sorry for him, seeing the hurt, wounded
look in his eyes and the pain in his face.

Who knows what was in her mind?
Perhaps she had seen the Master as they led Him in and felt
the irresistible attraction of the Great Galilean.

Perhaps in that brief moment, as they had crowded past her,
He had looked at her.
If He had—then something may have happened to her,
within her own heart.
Her faith might have been born,
A fire kindled by the spark that the winds of strange
circumstances had blown from the altar fires in the heart of
the Son of God.

Perhaps she wanted to ask Peter more about the Master.
Perhaps she would have said—had Peter acknowledged
Him:
> "Tell me the sound of His voice.
> Is it low and sweet, vibrant?
> Tell me of some of His miracles.
> Tell me how you are sure He is the Messiah.
> What is this salvation He speaks about?
> How can we live forever?"

Maybe these questions would have come tumbling in a
torrent from her lips . . . who knows?

But whatever she meant, whatever her motive for asking the
question,
  "Art not thou also one of this man's disciples?"
Peter denied his Lord and said: "I am not."

We can only stand aghast at Peter and wonder if the strain
and the shock have destroyed his memory.

Simon, surely you remember the first day you saw Him.
  Andrew and yourself floating the folded net . . . His
  shadow falling across you as you worked.
Don't you remember His command, His beckoning finger,
the light in His eyes, as He said: "Follow me, and *I will make
you fishers of men"*?

Peter, don't you remember?

And that night when Nicodemus came into the garden
looking for the Master. . . .
Don't you remember how he crept in with his cloak pulled
up over his face?
Don't you remember how he frightened you, and how
the Lord and Nicodemus talked for hours about the
promises?

Don't you remember the wedding in Cana where He turned
the water into wine?
Don't you remember the music of His laugh and the Samar-
itan woman at Sychar?
Don't you remember these things, Simon? . . .

And now they brought the Lord from Annas to Caiaphas,
and the soldiers and the Temple guards mingled with the
servants in the courtyard.

Because the night was cold, they had kindled a fire in the
brazier, and Peter joined himself to the group and, stretching
out his hands, warmed himself at their fire.

Peter was glad to join the hangers-on huddled around the blaze, for the morning air bit sharply, and he found himself shivering . . .
It was a kindly glow of warmth.

Coarse laughter greeted every joke and they discussed the things such people talk about:
    the prowess of the garrison's chariot drivers
        the gambling losses of their friends
            the new actor from Antioch at Herod's court
                the additional water tax just levied
                    the latest gossip from Rome.

Peter was not paying much attention to their conversation until one of the soldiers nudged him and said:
    "Thou art also of them."
And Peter said, for the second time: "Man, *I am not.*"

Peter, you must remember . . . surely . . . it must be that you are afraid.

Your brave heart must have turned to water.
Surely you cannot have forgotten. . . .
Many a time . . . crossing the lake in boats like your own,
    with its high seats
        its patched sails slanting in the sun
            and its thick oars?
Remember the night He came walking on the water, and you tried it, and were walking like the Master, until your courage left you . . . your faith gave way?

Simon, has your courage left you again?

Have you forgotten the pool at Bethesda and how you
laughed when the impotent man rose . . . rolled up his bed
   threw it over his shoulder
      and went away leaping in the air and shouting?

Ah, Simon, you spoke so bravely . . . and now here you are.

For the next hour or so they merely waited.
What was keeping them so long?
They little knew the difficulty of getting witnesses to agree.
They little knew that sleepless men, with tempers raw and
irritated, were trying to find some reason they could submit
to Pilate that would justify their demands for the death of
Jesus.

After an hour had passed, there joined the group a soldier
who had come out of the palace.
As he greeted his friends in the circle, his eye fell on Peter.
He scrutinized him very carefully, and Peter, feeling the
examination of the newcomer, looked around as the soldier
asked: "Did not I see thee in the garden with him?"

One of his friends joined in:
   "Certainly—he's one of the Galileans.
   Just listen to his accent."

And the soldier stubbornly went on: "I am sure I saw him in
the garden, for my kinsman Malchus was wounded by one
of them who drew a sword . . .
And if I am not mistaken—it was this fellow here."

Then Peter, beginning to curse and to swear, said:
   "I know not the man."

He used language he had not used for years.
It was vile . . . even the soldiers were shocked.
They all looked at him in amazement.

They did not appear to notice the shuffling of feet, as soldiers
led Christ from Caiaphas to Pilate.
Perhaps they did not make much noise.
They were tired, worn with argument and talk, so they were
very quiet.

The group standing 'round the fire was silent, shocked at the
vehemence and the profanity of Peter's denial.
It was a torrent of foulness, but it was his face that
startled them.
It was livid
        distorted
      eyes blazing
   mouth snarling like a cornered animal.
It was not a pleasant sight, and they kept silent.
It was a silence so intense that the crowing of a distant cock
was like a bugle call. . . .

Immediately, Peter remembered the Lord's prophecy:
   "Before the cock crow, thou shalt deny me thrice."

Like a wave there swept over him the realization of what he
had done.

With tears streaming down his face, he turned away from the fire.

Ahead of him he saw the stairway that led to Pilate's palace. . . .
And by a terrible Providence, it was just at that moment that Christ was being led up the stairs to appear before Pilate.

The Lord had heard!
The Lord had heard every hot, searing word. . . .
The Lord had heard the blistering denial . . . the foul fisherman's oaths. . . .
He—He had heard it all!

Christ paused on the stair, and looked down over the rail—
   looked right into the very soul of Peter.
The eyes of the two met . . . at that awful moment.

Through his tears all else was a blur to Peter.
But that one face shone through the tears . . .
   that lovely face
      that terrible face
         those eyes—sad, reproachful, tender . . . as if they
         understood and forgave.

Ah, how well he knew Him, and how much he loved Him.

The world seemed to stand still as, for that terrible moment, Peter looked at the One he had denied.

We shall never know what passed between them.
Christ seemed to say again:

"But I have prayed for thee, Simon,
Satan hath desired to have thee,
But I have prayed for thee."

Simon's tears now overflowed and ran down his cheeks—
            hot and scalding tears they were—
And with great sobs shaking his strong frame, he spun
'round and rushed out to where the cool morning air might
fan his burning cheeks.

He fled with his heart pounding in his breast, while the
Nazarene walked steadily to meet the Roman governor.

"Then assembled together the chief priests, and
the scribes, and the elders of the people, unto the
palace of the high priest, who was called Caiaphas,
And consulted that they might take Jesus by subt-
ilty, and kill Him.

"But they said, Not on the feast day, lest there be an
uproar among the people."

Why did the religionists of Jesus' time want to kill Him?
Why was Caiaphas in particular anxious to get Him out of
the way?
What was the charge against the Nazarene?

The Sadducees were the religious elite of the day.
Not only was Caiaphas, the present high priest, a Sadducee,
but he was also the son-in-law of Annas, now an old man,

whom he had succeeded in that office.

Now that Palestine was under Roman jurisdiction, even the high priest was a Roman appointee.

But so crafty a politician was Annas that Caiaphas was the seventh member of his own family to receive the coveted appointment.

Both were wealthy men.

The Temple—the religious domain over which they presided—was also a financial empire.

By a rare financial strategy, they had made it so.

Annas and Caiaphas controlled the market in the Temple porch, where sacrifices were sold to pilgrim worshipers and Roman money was exchanged for the statutory half-shekel required as a Temple offering.

The priests determined the rate of exchange and made money shamelessly.

Moreover, they drew rent from the ground on which the sellers of animals for sacrifice put up their stalls and stacked their dove cages.

The people knew this and resented it, but what could they do?

What can the general populace ever do about taxes that eat up the fat of the land?

An income equivalent to millions of dollars a year was flowing into the Temple treasuries.

Jesus knew all this; it was common knowledge.

No wonder His indignation was aroused, especially when

this evil was carried on in the name of worship of the living
God.

The most scathing words He ever uttered were spoken
against the men who perpetrated this wholesale theft.
The scathing words had come to the ears of Annas and
Caiaphas.
For many months they had had spies reporting back to them
on the itinerant preacher.
Exactly how dangerous was He?
The day came when the Nazarene strode into the Temple
court and overthrew the tables of the moneychangers.
That dynamic figure had stridden about among the mer-
chants, unafraid.
The folds of His robe falling away from His right arm had
revealed powerful muscles.
Angry priests had stood helplessly by,
    muttering threats in throaty growls. . . .

The moneychangers had screamed in frenzy
    as they had groveled among the filth to retrieve their
    coins that had rolled in a hundred directions.
And the pilgrims who had been bled white all these years
had laughed and added their own shouts of encourage-
ment.

Minutes later an observer had run to tell the servant of the
high priest.

But Caiaphas was afraid of the common people and dared
not intervene.

For the popularity of this Jesus was largely with the common folk.

Stories of His wonderful works were everywhere.

The beggars in the streets talked of them . . .

They were discussed by the drivers of the caravans at every stop . . .

And the stories lost nothing in the telling.

It was said that He healed the blind.

There were cripples who had thrown away their crutches.

There was a current story about a little girl who had been dead and had been restored to her father.

And now the latest story—

the one about Lazarus, a prominent citizen, indeed a wealthy man of Bethany, being brought back to life. . . .

Caiaphas had secretly checked and rechecked.

That task had not been too difficult, because Bethany was so close.

He had been unable to find anyone to refute the story—

It was so odd!

Enough to make a man uneasy—

With such power and a growing following, anything could happen.

No wonder the chief priests and the Pharisees got together and asked:

"What shall we do? for this man doeth many miracles. If we let Him thus alone, all men will believe on

Him; And the Romans shall come and take away
both our place and nation."

Caiaphas was the one who suggested a solution.
Only the Romans could execute a death sentence.
Surely it was useless to settle for less.
Nothing else would finally silence the Galilean.

Therefore the crux of the problem was to find a charge
against Jesus that would satisfy Roman law.

The high priest well knew that if the true Messiah should
ever come, there would be two immediate results . . .
  The political supremacy of Rome would be challenged
  by revolt. This would mean Rome's suppression of the
  revolt by violence,
                and
  The Messiah, if accepted by the people, would usurp
  Caiaphas' own position and power.

Did not this Jesus claim to be the Messiah?
Then this was the perfect charge. . . .
So Caiaphas argued to the priests:
  " 'It is expedient for you that one man should die for the
  people, and that the whole nation perish not.'. . .
  *From that day forth, they took counsel that they might put
  Him to death."*

And now, with Judas' help, it had come.
The Nazarene,

His hands bound with ropes,
His face and beard matted with blood from the blows of
the soldiers . . .
stood before him.

The court had been hastily convened in the middle of the
night.
Some of Caiaphas' colleagues might have been drowsy and
half-asleep at that time, but the high priest was thoroughly
alert.

For hours he had been busy getting word to the seventy
members of the Sanhedrin . . .
   trying to round up men who would testify against
   Christ.
Haste was important.

The members of the Sanhedrin sat on stone seats in a
three-tiered semicircle.
Some seats were vacant; it was still an hour before dawn.
Witness after witness came forward.
But the witnesses could not agree among themselves
and the prisoner refused to say anything.
As soon as one spoke against Jesus, another contradicted
and a great tumult broke out.

Caiaphas grew red in the face with mounting frustration. He
had already risked much to bring Jesus to trial:

   It was illegal for the Temple guard, acting under the orders
   of the high priest, to arrest the prisoner.

The arrest should have been made spontaneously by the witnesses.

It was clearly against the law to try a capital charge at night.

Finally Caiaphas, having utterly failed with his witnesses, knew that nothing that had been said could give the color of justice to the sentence of death.

He rose from his seat and walked over to where he could look down into the calm face of the prisoner.

If witnesses could not condemn Him, he must try to get Him to condemn Himself.

Turning to the Nazarene, the judge addressed Him:
    "Answerest Thou nothing to the things which these witnesses say against Thee?"

But Jesus held His peace.

The silence angered the high priest.

He seemed ready to explode.

The jewels on his robes sparkled and flashed in the light from the bronze lamps, as his eyes flashed anger.

And then, with all the authority he could crowd into the words, Caiaphas put to Jesus the solemn Jewish oath of testimony:

    "I adjure Thee by the living God. . . ."

When a question was put like that to a loyal Jew, it was an offense not to answer.

Caiaphas was asking a question that really mattered—
    a question that required an answer clear-cut, like chiseled marble—

And the question rang out through the assembly:
> "I adjure Thee by the living God, that Thou tell us
> whether Thou be the Christ, the Son of God."

Priests and rabbis
   scribes
      Pharisees and Sadducees
         learned men of Israel . . .
They all knew what the question meant.

They sprang to their feet in the excitement, craning forward
to catch the reply.
Would the Nazarene reply?
If He kept His silence, then the Sanhedrin would have no
choice but to release Him.
His life hung on His answer. . . .

Once again Jesus took the initiative on His road to the cross.
He would answer!
His voice rang out.
There are three versions of His reply in the Gospels!

Mark writes it: "I am."
   Matthew writes it: "Thou hast said."
      Luke writes it: "Ye say that I am. . . ."

The meaning is the same.
There was no doubt in the mind of the high priest as to what
Jesus' reply signified.
At last he had triumphed.

He swung 'round on the assembled rabbis, tearing his robe
from top to bottom, according to custom.

His voice shrill with victory, he shouted:

> "What further need have we of witnesses?"

The charge of blasphemy had been established.

It was sufficient.

The Sanhedrin had no choice but to impose the solemn sentence:

> "He is liable to be put to death."

The Roman procurator, Pontius Pilate, was not in the best of moods.

He did not relish having to rise at cockcrow to try a case.

These Jewish people over whom Caesar had sent him to rule four years earlier were a difficult, turbulent race.

The army of occupation was forever trying to keep the lid on a smoldering volcano.

Pilate had a soldier's contempt for religion.

Of course, it was true that he was superstitious—

some unexpected event . . .

some omen . . .

a dream . . .

the pronouncement of some oracle . . .

the voice of a soothsayer in the marketplace . . .

the cast of the dice . . .

These could cause him to tremble.

But as for religion . . .

Well, he had seen many religions—

in Egypt and Persia, through Asia Minor and Macedonia—

And they all seemed alike to him.

No prayers and mystic rites could stand up against the Roman legions.

As for him, give him a legion of hardy veterans . . .

shining armor . . .
flashing spears . . .
trusty swords . . .

And a fig for all the religions in the world!

Yet these religious Jews baffled him—irritated him.
He had tried putting them down by force.
There had been the affair of the money he had taken from the sacred treasury to better Jerusalem's water supply, and the bloody revolt that had followed.
And that incident of the votive shields in the Herodian palace. . . .

Yes, he had tried riding roughshod over their prejudices.
And the moment he had touched their religion, they had risen defenseless as sheep but as angry as wolves.
It was all so illogical and absurd!
Such may well have been his thoughts as he strode through the outer door of the Praetorium toward this unpleasant early-morning hearing.

The Roman paused at the head of the marble staircase.
With cool scrutiny he regarded the crowd before him.
On his shaven face with its keen eyes there was just a trace of a sneer, for he had been told that the Jews had ceremonial objections to treading the stones of the Gentile palace lest they be made unclean for the Passover.
So he, Pilate, must go out to them.

Grimly, he gathered his purple-bordered toga over his arm
and strode down the steps.
The seething mass of humanity before him seemed centered
around one solitary Man who was being thrust forward.
Pilate's first impression was that He was perfectly harmless.
He looked Him over with the eyes of a trained soldier.
He looked first for a sign of weapons. . . . There was none.

The prisoner was dressed in a simple white robe,
                              open at the neck,
     wrinkled and soiled from rough handling.
His hands were bound behind His back.
Pilate then looked for confederates or friends of the prisoner.
There were none.

Many of the faces before him were livid.
The crowd looked like a pack of snarling animals.
The Roman governor raised his baton as a signal that the trial
could begin and asked:
"What accusation bring ye against this man?"

The reply was insolent . . .
"If He were not an evildoer we would not have delivered
Him up unto thee."

Once more Pilate looked at the prisoner.
An evildoer?
If the Roman was any judge of men—
     and he prided himself on that—
this prisoner was no vicious character.
"Take Him away," he said, turning to go back into the palace.

"Take Him away and deal with Him according to
your own law."

Now a veritable howl went up . . .
"It is not lawful for us to put any man to death."

Ah, so that was what they wanted . . .
The blood-lust was in their eyes.
He knew now what the Jews wanted of him—to make
convenience of his rank and position . . .
And woe be to him if he blocked their intentions.

Pilate hesitated.
Once more his eyes rested on the prisoner.

His was the only calm face in that seething sea—
                                    and what a face it was!
There was something in the eyes . . .
    in the set of the mouth . . .
        something about the bearing that was different—
                                            strange
                                            compelling.

There came to the Roman governor an instinctive desire to
get away from the crowd,
    to be alone with this Man and speak with Him face-to-face.

So he turned and strode back into the palace and sat down
upon the dais.
Then he gave command that the prisoner be brought before
him.

Quietly and with stately mien, Jesus—the chiliarch of the
Twelfth Legion beside Him—walked across the mosaic floor
until He stood in front of the powerful Roman, and turned
His deep, searching eyes upon him.

Outside of the narrow pointed windows the sound of the
impatient murmuring of the crowd was wafted into
the Judgment Hall.
Pilate paid no attention.
His hands rested on the gilded carving of the bisellium.
His eyes narrowed as they stared moodily at the white-robed
figure before him.

For a moment there was silence.
Then Pilate's involuntary question surprised even himself:

     "Art Thou the King of the Jews?"

A faint smile came over the face of Jesus . . .
     "Sayest thou this thing of thyself, or did others tell
     it thee concerning Me?"

It was the first time that Pilate had heard the Man's voice.
He did not say so, but it was the prisoner's deportment that
had made him involuntarily associate kingliness with Him.
     "Am I a Jew?" he asked contemptuously.
     "Thine own nation and the chief priests have
     delivered Thee unto me. Tell me—what hast
     Thou done?"

A faraway look came into the eyes of Christ.
He seemed to be seeing into the far distances.
He had done many things in three short years.

He had never hurried;
yet He had been conscious of time fleeting.
And He had warned His disciples that the night cometh
when no man can work.

Yet the seed had been sown.
Eleven men had been impregnated with the Gospel.
The increase would come in due time.
His task was almost finished now.
Only one great act remained, and it was moving swiftly
toward its climax.

What had He done?
No crime certainly—no political misdemeanor.
Had He not told John's messengers:

> ". . . The blind receive their sight, and the lame
> walk, and the lepers are cleansed, and the deaf hear,
> and the dead are raised up, and the poor have the
> Gospel preached unto them"?

That was something. . . .
But Pilate would not be interested in that.

So He said gently:

> "My Kingdom is not of this world: if My Kingdom
> were of this world, then would My servants fight,
> that I should not be delivered to the Jews: but now
> is My Kingdom not from hence."

Pilate persisted:

> "Art Thou a king then?"

Anything less like a king—judged by his own standards—*could hardly be imagined,* thought Pilate.

The prisoner stood before him alone, without a single person to plead His cause.

He stood there arrayed in a plain, seamless, soiled robe, the dress of a peasant.

Here at any rate was no king whom Caesar need fear.

"My Kingdom is not of this world," Jesus had said.

His Kingdom did not belong to the same order of things as Caesar's kingdom.

Therefore, the two could never come into collision.

His Kingdom was a repudiation of all political aims.

It was a flat denial of the insinuations made by the priests that the Nazarene was plotting treason.

But it was an assertion that claimed kingship of some sort . . .

So Pilate probed further. . . .

"So Thou art a king then?"

And Jesus nodded.

"Thou sayest. . . . To this end have I been born, that I should bear witness unto the truth. Every one that is of the truth heareth My voice."

Pilate seemed a little weary of the interview.

He had learned what he wanted to know—

this man was harmless.

"What is truth?" he asked.

Then, without waiting for a reply, he rose and went outside
to give his answer to the impatient Jews.
He held up his baton for silence.
In a ringing voice he said:
        "I find no fault with this man."

The chief priests were now more angry than ever.
They spat out their accusations . . .

        "He stirreth up the people.
        He teacheth throughout all Jewry,
        beginning from Galilee to this place. . . ."

The word *Galilee* leaped out at Pilate.
He saw a possible loophole . . .

        "Is this man from Galilee?"

When the priests answered in the affirmative, he said firmly:
        "Then send the prisoner to Herod.
        I cannot try this case. It is not in my jurisdiction."

And Pilate thought that he had dismissed the matter,
    was well rid of an embarrassing issue.
The New Testament narratives leave no doubt that
what Pilate most wanted was to find a way to release Christ.

But Christ before Herod was a greater enigma to the Jewish
ruler than to the Roman.
Herod expected to see Him do some tricks, for the stories of
His miracles had long since been trickling into the court.
The Jewish king was eager for a command performance.

But Jesus stood, silently eloquent.
He had nothing to say—nothing, that is, to Herod.
So Herod sent Him back to Pilate.

The howlings for His death now became even more
vehement.
And Pilate, supremely weary now of the whole matter, sat,
chin in hand, on his curule chair—
 the cobalt-blue chair of judgment under the
 movable canopy—
gloomily watching the yelling mob.
At that moment, a cohort bowed before him.
   "Sire, an urgent message. . . ."
And he handed the Roman a thin wax tablet.

It was a message from Pilate's wife—Claudia.
Pilate frowned, because never before had Claudia inter-
rupted him in the midst of a hearing.
Ordinarily, she would have not dared.
The message was the more urgent for its brevity:

   "Have thou nothing to do with that just man:
   for I have suffered many things this day
   in a dream because of Him."

Pilate's thoughts went back to the night before . . .
 the nocturnal visit of the high priest. . . .
Claudia had questioned him after the high priest had left.
Husband and wife had quarreled a bit. . . .

   "It isn't really like you—a Roman—to agree
   to a man's death ahead of time.

I have seen this man in the streets of Jerusalem,
watched Him once for minutes on end from my
litter.
He seems harmless enough. I don't like this affair."

Pilate had slipped out that morning at cockcrow without
waking Claudia—
Now this—the Roman procurator's hand trembled a bit.
Dreams made him uneasy.
Warnings *could* come that way.
Perhaps Claudia was right after all. . . .

Pilate leaned forward intently in his chair.

"Ye have brought this man unto me, as one that
perverteth the people: and, behold, I,
having examined Him before you, have found
no fault in this man touching those things
whereof ye accuse Him:

"No, nor yet Herod: for I sent you to him; and lo,
nothing worthy of death is done unto Him.

"I will therefore chastise Him, and release Him."

But the whole multitude burst into a shout,

"Away with this man! If you release any,
release Barabbas."

Pilate shouted, "Barabbas is a robber and murderer.
What harm has this Jesus done?"

But the mob would not listen.
Prompted by the priests, they shouted, "Crucify . . .

> crucify . . .
>
> crucify. . . ."

In a chant that beat with unreasoning insistence
and rose and fell like the waves of an angry sea.

The procurator could scarcely make himself heard.
He stood outwardly patient,
  his lips curling,
    and an ugly look in his eyes. . . .

> "Would you have me crucify your king?"

That enraged them the more. . . .

> "We have no king but Caesar."

Desperately Pilate tried once more.
He held up his baton. . . .

> "I know it is your custom to have a man released at
> your Festival. There is nothing in this Jesus that
> deserves death. If it will please you, I shall scourge
> Him and let Him go."

But the mob would not have it so.
Then the voice of Caiaphas rose high and clear
above the clamor:

> "Any man who sets himself up as a king is a rebel
> against Caesar. . . ."

The clear insinuation was, "Do you want me to get word back to Rome that you have encouraged rebellion against Caesar?"

And now Pilate motioned for Jesus to be brought closer to the curule chair.

In some strange way this Nazarene had impressed him.

Perhaps it was the look in His eyes.
It was something that made Pilate feel uncomfortable.

Of course the Roman governor had seen many zealots.
He had grown accustomed to them.
Down from the hill country they would bring an insurrectionist . . . with blazing eyes . . . wild, twitching mouth . . .
Or men with pinpoints of fire for eyes . . .
    and hatred smoldering for the emblems of Rome . . .
Or some poor devils caught in the toils of religious bigotry.
He used to watch them in a detached way with a sneer in his heart.

But this was different.
He had spoken to this prisoner, and it made him
the more uncertain.

He had a curious feeling that Claudia was right; there was more in this than met the eye.
Surely he was enough of a politician to find some loophole, some way to handle this curious case.

He addressed himself to the prisoner:
        "Whence art Thou?"

But Jesus only looked at him straight in the eyes
and said nothing.
The silence puzzled Pilate.
The prisoner had talked to him inside the Judgment Hall.
Why not now?

> "Speakest Thou not unto me? Knowest Thou not
> that I have power to crucify Thee, and have power to
> release Thee?"

It was almost as if Pilate were saying,
"Only say the word, and I shall release You.
Only tell me that You are no insurrectionist. . . ."
And so, once again, Christ could have escaped the cross—
But He would not. . . .

And so Jesus answered—slowly—clearly—

> "Thou couldest have no power at all against Me,
> except it were given thee from above: therefore, he
> that delivered Me unto thee hath the greater sin."

Christ's words did not irritate Pilate.
He squared his shoulders, all the more determined to find a
way to release the Nazarene.

But now the sea of humanity before him
  took up the cry again . . .
> "Crucify . . .
>   crucify . . .
>   crucify. . . ."

The tumult was beyond all control, and a guard of soldiers
moved nearer Pilate—just in case—

But he waved them back, and spoke to an attendant who
hurried inside.

Pilate stood there waiting, unable to hide his contempt.
The prisoner before him was pale and very tired, swaying a
bit on His feet.
The Roman looked over His head to the priests—
                    seeing the hate in their eyes
                    hearing the savagery of their shouting,
and he found himself wondering about their religion . . .
    marveling at any religion that would permit them
    to behave like this.

By this time a servant returned bearing a basin of water and
a towel.
Pilate, unable to make himself heard at all now, wanted to
dramatize something.
Deliberately, in sight of them all,
    slowly he washed his hands . . .
        slowly dried them.

Now the tumult gradually died.
Then he stepped forward and said clearly and deliberately:
        "I am innocent of the blood of this just man. See ye
        to it!"

And with loud shouts of triumph, the people yelled:
        "His blood be on us and on our children."

Pilate shuddered involuntarily.
He had tried . . . he could tell Claudia he had tried.

Perhaps, by washing his hands, he had dispelled the evil omen.

His last act, before turning Jesus over to be scourged and crucified, was to write the inscription to be put over His cross

in Latin

in Greek

and in Hebrew:

"Jesus of Nazareth the King of the Jews."

When Caiaphas saw it, he remonstrated:

"That is no accusation. People will not understand. Do not write 'The King of Jews,' but that He said, 'I am King of the Jews.' "

But Pilate answered bitterly, almost spitting out each word:

"What I have written I have written."

And from a distant courtyard there came the sound of a flagellum, into which had been fastened bits of lead and glass and bone and chain, striking again and again the bared back of the Nazarene.

The little man Judas had followed the crowd to the courtyard of the Fortress Antonia.

Slinking, keeping well to the fringe of the screaming mob, he

had watched with mounting horror the sequence of events.
When the farce of a trial had finally reached its climax
and Judas had heard the mob shouting:

"His blood be on us and on our children,"
he had gathered his robes about him, and turned fleeing.

How could he have known it would turn out like this?
He had so hoped that his action would force the Master's
hand,
    force Him to go ahead and establish His earthly
    kingdom . . .
But crucifixion? Not *that!*

The thirty pieces of silver in the leather purse dangling
around his waist seemed to be burning his thighs.
This was now blood money.
Somehow, some way he must get rid of it. . . .
He raced through the narrow twisting streets toward the
Temple, dodging people and donkeys as he went.
Once he almost collided with a man carrying a basket of figs,
and the man swore loudly at his retreating figure.

In the Temple he asked a doorkeeper to see the chief priest.
"Through that room and along the colonnade to the right,"
the doorkeeper said.
Then, noting Judas' wild eyes, "No, wait—let me see—"
but already the wild one was racing toward the colonnade.

Judas burst into a room where some of the elders
were assembled.

His hands clutched convulsively at the moneybag swinging
at his waist.
His eyes were bloodshot.
"I have sinned," he said.

Eyebrows went up; there were questions in the eyes.
The elders noted that this strange man was panting.

"I have sinned in that I have betrayed innocent blood. . . .
You know—Jesus of Nazareth. He had done nothing amiss.
I did not know that. . . ."

Shoulders shrugged.
Sardonic smiles appeared on some of the faces.
   "Jesus of Nazareth? Oh, yes—that one.
Well—what is that to us? See thou to that. . . ."

Judas could not believe what he had just heard.
Then the truth dawned on him.
The fate of Christ was already out of the hands of these men;
moreover, they didn't *care* . . .
The Master was going to die after all. . . .

There was nothing he could do about it. . . .

With trembling hands he seized the coin purse and opened
it.
Slowly he counted out thirty pieces of silver.
Once again he looked questioningly into the eyes of the
elders standing before him.

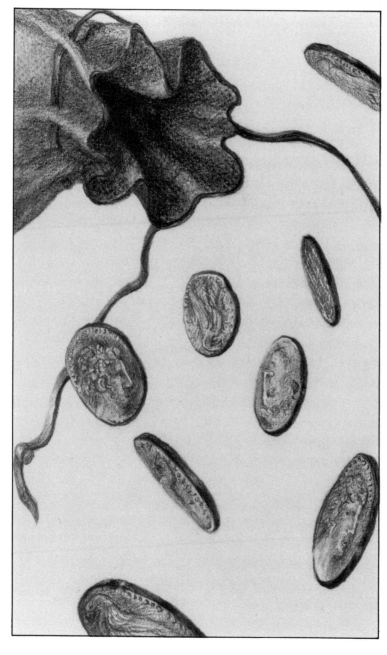

He saw only amusement—
With a contemptuous gesture Judas flung the silver at them
                              right into their faces.
They ducked the shower of silver, and the coins fell to the
marble floor, rolling in all directions.
Then Judas turned and fled from the room.

The little man did not stop running until he was outside the
city gates.
A picture kept flashing before his eyes—he brushed his
hands before his eyes but it would not leave.
It was Jesus' face at that moment when he, Judas, had kissed
His cheek.

"Friend," He had said gently, "wherefore art thou come?
Why have you done this?"

"Friend," that was what He had said. "Friend—why have
you done this?"
                    It broke Judas' heart. . . .

His plan had failed.
Everything was smashed . . . his dreams . . . his hopes . . .
                    his life—everything.

There was nothing left—now.
Only one way out. . . .

A few hours later the body of Judas was found
swinging crazily from the branch of a tree on the precipitous
heights overlooking the Valley of the Hinnom.
He had died before the Master.

An orange morning sun was rising higher and higher
over the City of David.
Pilgrims and visitors for the feast were pouring in through
the gates, mingling with merchants from the villages
round-about,
     shepherds coming in from the hills,
   hucksters leading their laden camels in single file,
  donkeys standing sleepily beneath their burdens in the
  dappled sunlight.

The narrow streets were crowded.
There were the aged, stooped with years, muttering to
themselves as they pushed through the throngs.
There were children playing in the streets, calling to each
other in shrill voices.

And beggars raising sightless sockets to the sky,
                    tapping sticks on the cobblestones
                    demanding alms in nasal voices.

From every balcony and latticed window came
                    the sound of voices
                    scraps of laughter
                    rude voices, bargaining.

There were men and women carrying burdens . . .
                    baskets of vegetables
                    of green almonds and sweet lemons
                 casks of wine
               water bags.

There were cloth merchants with their bales.
Fruiterers were arranging their stalls in narrow bazaars striped with sunlight.
Tradesmen with their tools seemed out-of-place in the holiday atmosphere.

It was not easy to make one's way through the crowd.

It was especially difficult for the procession that started out from the governor's palace.

At its head rode Longenius, the Roman centurion in charge of a half-maniple of the famous Twelfth Legion.
He seemed a typical Roman, scornful alike of child or cripple who might be in his way.

Before him went two legionnaires, one of them carrying a board atop a pole in which had been printed the charges against those to be executed.
The legionnaires were clearing the crowd aside as best they could, with curses and careless blows.

The procession moved at a snail's pace.
The soldiers tried to keep step.
The centurion's guard evidently did not relish this routine task, which came to them every now and then in the governing of this troublesome province.

The sunlight glanced on the spears and helmets of the soldiers.
There was a clanking of steel as their shields touched their belt buckles and the scabbards of their swords.

Between the two files of soldiers staggered three condemned men, each carrying a heavy bar of wood with its crosspiece, on which he was to be executed.

It was hard to keep step, for the pace was slow, and the soldiers were impatient to get it over.
Left . . . right . . . left . . . right . . .
In sharp clipped commands they urged their prisoners on.

The crosses were heavy, and the first of the victims was at the point of collapse.
He had been under severe strain for several days.
He had eaten little and had not closed His eyes for two days.
Moreover, the lashing with the flagellum had taken the last bit of His strength.

The carpenter followed them, with his ladder and his nails, and they all moved forward out of the courtyard of Pilate's palace toward the Gennath Gate.

The orange sun was hot.
The sweat poured down the face of Jesus, and He swayed now and then under the weight of the cross.
A depression had fallen on the soldiers, and they marched in silence, as if reluctantly.

A group of women went with the procession, their faces half-hidden by their veils, but their grief could not be hidden.
Some were sobbing . . .
   Others were praying . . .

Others were moaning in that deep grief that knows not what it says or does.

Some of them had children by the hand and kept saying over and over . . .
"He gave my child back to me . . .
How can they be so cruel?
I know He healed my child—
What harm could there be in that?"

And there were men, too, who followed as closely as they could—men who walked with the strange steps of those to whom walking was unfamiliar.
They were the cripples He had healed.

Others carried sticks in their hands—sticks that once had tapped out their blind tattoo along the city streets and the sun-hardened trails of Judea.

They did not use their sticks now, although once again they were blind . . . blinded by tears.

Once when the procession halted for a moment, Jesus turned and spoke to them, but they could not hear Him for the shouting of the rabble.

Most of the crowd hardly knew what was going on.
They did not understand.
They caught the infection of the mob spirit.

They shouted to the first of three victims.

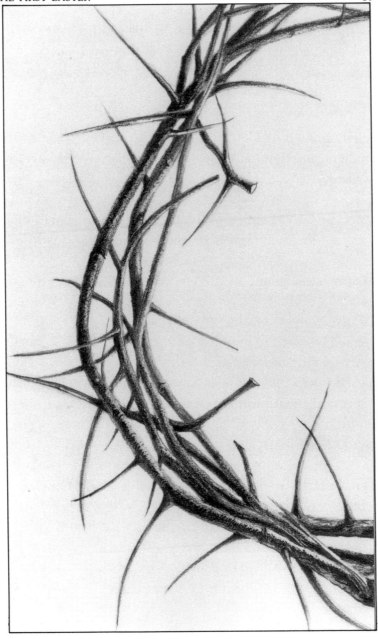

That one had an absurd crown on His head,
  twisted from a branch of the long-thorned briar.
It had lacerated His scalp and caused blood to mingle with
the sweat.

They shouted at Him, until roughly pushed aside by the
soldiers, and then, in some cases, they began to shout at the
soldiers.

It was an ugly situation as the procession went slowly along
this way that will forever be known as the Via Dolorosa.

Meanwhile—Simon of Cyrene was approaching the city
gate.

He had just arrived in Judea, and was about to enter the holy
city as a pilgrim for the festival.
He had spent the night in some village just outside, and,
rising early that morning, had bathed and dressed himself
carefully . . . with a tingling excitement because soon he
would be in Jerusalem.

The wonders of Jerusalem, that exiles had described, he
would now see with his own eyes.
The sounds of the holy city which lonely hearts heard in
their nostalgia . . .
  Noises that seemed to be whispered by the restless surf of
  distant seas, or heard in the moaning of winds that
  traveled far . . .
These he would hear with his own ears.

Yet he tried to keep calm, and as he set out on the short walk
that lay between him and the city, he was very thoughtful.

He walked along the winding path that sometimes ran
through the fields . . .
    sometimes along narrow roads between hedges where
        there was the fragrance of pomegranate trees and hon-
        eysuckle . . .
    sometimes along the tortuous course of the dried-up river
        bed where the earth was cracked with the heat of the
        sun.

Sometimes it wound up the jagged hillside to twist down
among the giant boulders and huge rocks behind which
many a robber might hide.
He walked along beside the tall rushes, where he frightened
coveys of birds that flew wheeling, diving . . .
And he walked through the divided crops, ripening in the
sunshine.

He could hear the sheep bleating on the inhospitable hillside,
while the morning sun climbed higher and chased away the
mists that lay in the hollows, trailing down into the ravines
like tulle scarves.

As he walked along, he was thinking of the Temple and its
glories, the history of his people and the worship of his
fathers . . .
Already he could see ahead of him the domes of the Temple
gleaming gold in the sunshine, could hear the pigeons that
had their nests in the cupolas and gables,

And he thought of his own city looking from her height over the blue waters of the Mediterranean.

Then as he neared the city gate he began to hear shouting that grew louder and louder.
There seemed to Simon to be a sort of chant running through the noise . . .
  a refrain that men's voices made clearer and clearer until he thought he could recognize the word
    "Crucify
   crucify
     crucify. . . ."
They met right at the city gate . . . Simon of Cyrene and the crowd.

He found that the procession was headed by some Roman soldiers; he would recognize them anywhere . . .
    the insignia on their shields . . .
  and their uniforms . . .
He could tell a legionnaire when he saw one.

He had little time to gather impressions, and as for asking questions, that was impossible.
He could not make himself heard in all the rabble.
The noise and confusion with its sinister malice made Simon shudder.
Simon was aware of two moving walls of Roman steel.

There was something strange about it all but, before he could understand it, Simon was caught up in it—sucked into the procession, and swept out through the gate again.

Simon was excited, afraid. . . .
He was puzzled and ill-at-ease.
He scanned face after face quickly, looking for some light of
pity . . .
    of friendliness
        of welcome . . .
But he found none.

He felt the drama of the situation, the cruelty of it . . .
And its horror crept over him like a clammy mist—and he
shivered.

He was captured by the procession, stumbling along tightly
wedged in the very heart of the crowd.
Then he noticed that there were three men who staggered
under the weight of crosses of rough, heavy wood on which
these unfortunates were going to die.

Each man was bent beneath the burden he carried, and
perspiration moistened his drawn face.
One of them was strangely appealing, His face arresting.
Simon felt his gaze returning again and again to that one
face.
He noticed that blood was trickling down from wounds in
the brow.

On His face there was a twig of long-thorned briar, twisted
around in the shape of a crown and pushed down cruelly on
His head.

Simon watched with beating heart as they shuffled along,
fascinated by the look in those eyes.

He could see nothing else.
Everything was forgotten, even why he had come to Jerusalem.

This public execution had driven everything else from his mind.

Forgotten for the moment were the Temple and its services,
    messages he brought from friends far away . . .
        things he had been asked to get . . .
Everything was forgotten as he watched this Man carrying the cross.

And then *He* looked up! His eyes almost blinded by the blood that trickled down from under that grotesque crown that was on His head. . . .
Why didn't somebody wipe His eyes?

And as Simon looked at Him, He looked at Simon . . .
And the eyes of the two . . . met!
How did Christ know what was in Simon's heart?
What was it that made Him smile, a slow, sad smile that seemed to still Simon's wildly beating heart and give him courage?

The look that passed between them Simon never forgot as long as he lived, for no man can look at Jesus of Nazareth and remain the same.

As these two looked at each other, the Man with the cross stumbled, and the soldiers, moved more by impatience than

pity, seeing the Nazarene was almost too exhausted to carry
the cross any further, laid hands on Simon and conscripted
him to carry it.

He was the nearest man.
He was strong.
His shoulders were broad!

Simon's heart almost stopped beating; he tried to speak, but
no words came.
A few minutes before, he had been a lonely pilgrim quietly
approaching the holy city.
And now, here he was in the midst of a procession of
howling men and women, walking between two moving
walls of Roman steel, and carrying on his shoulder a cross on
which someone was going to die!

The look of gratitude and love that flashed from the eyes of
Jesus as Simon lifted the load from those tired, bleeding
shoulders did something to the man from Cyrene, and in an
instant life was changed.

Simon never could explain it afterward—how it happened!

There are moments of spiritual insight that defy the limits of
syntax and grammar.
There are experiences that can never be poured into the
molds of speech.
There are some things too deep for words.

But all at once he saw the meaning of pain . . .
    understood the significance of suffering. . . .

The meaning of prayer was unveiled . . .
    and the message of the Scriptures.
He saw prophecy take form and live before him.
He remembered words of the psalmist and the prophets of
old, words that until now had been without sense or
meaning,
but now . . . he saw . . . and understood.

And so the crowd came to Golgotha, a hill shaped like a
skull, outside the city gates, where two great highways, the
Samaria-Jerusalem road and the Joppa-Jerusalem road, con-
verged upon the city.

Only as the nails were driven in did the shouting stop.
There was a hush.
    Most of them were stunned . . . horrified . . .
Even the hardest of them were silenced.

Mary, the mother of Jesus, closed her eyes and stopped her
ears; she could not bear the thud of the hammer.

Simon of Cyrene from time to time wiped away his tears
with the back of his hand.
Peter stood on the fringe of the crowd, blinded by hot tears
that filled his eyes, while his very heart broke.

A group of soldiers took hold of the crossbeam and lifted it
slowly off the ground.

With each movement the nails tore at the shredded flesh in
the wrists of the Nazarene.
The cross swayed in the air for a moment and then with a
thud dropped into the hole prepared for it.

When the first spasm of pain had waned, Jesus opened His
eyes.
Over the heads of the crowd, He could see the city, tawny-
yellow, like a crouching tiger in the midday sun.

Nearer there was a hillside carpeted with anemone and
cyclamen.
For just a moment a gentle spring wind blowing across the
face of the suffering Man blew away the smell of blood and
wafted to Him the fragrance of flowers, and He saw a single
lark circling high above the hillside.

But closer still a mad medley of fury surged below Him. . . .
There were eyes watching this Man on His cross . . .
     unbelieving eyes
          eyes with gloating in them
               other eyes that looked and never saw.

Faces were looking up at Him . . . convulsed faces,
     snarling, invective faces,
faces that through His pain-glazed eyes seemed to melt and
run together.

Fingers pointed up to Him hanging quivering on the cross-
gibbet . . .
     long bony fingers . . .

mocking, accusing fingers—fingers of scorn and ridicule.

There was noise . . . confused noise that beat upon His ears with an added pain.
There was demoniac laughter that enjoyed suffering.
There was hoarse shouting that taunted and mocked.

From one side of Him there were sighs of pain and the soft moans of a dying thief, and on the other side blasphemies and curses terrible to hear.
There was weeping too, the crying of the women and the unashamed sobbing of men.

The wounded flower of Magdala was consoled by that lovely one who had once held Him in her arms, while the beloved John stood beside them.

The crowd hurled His own words back at Him, but they were barbs, dipped in venom and shot from snarling lips, like poisoned arrows.

> "He saved others; Himself He cannot save.
> Yes, He healed the cripples.
> Yes, He gave sight to the blind.
> He even brought back the dead, but He cannot save Himself."

They were willing now to grant the truth of His miracles. Out of the mouths of His enemies comes this testimony to His power—"He saved others" . . .

Yes, they were saved—those others . . .

saved from the land of shadows
    saved from the caves of derangement
        from the couches of pain
        from the leprous touch of sickness
    saved from the enslaving grip of vice
  saved even from the jaws of death.
Yes, He had saved others—His enemies admitted it. . . .

But now their taunt rose to its crescendo—

> "Perform a miracle now, Miracle Man! Come down
> from the cross, and we will believe Thee.
> Aha, Thou who wouldst build the Temple in three
> days,
> Thou hast nails in Thy hands now . . .
> Thou hast wood . . . go on and build Thy Temple.
>
> "If Thou be the Christ . . . prove it to us . . . Come
> on down from the cross!"

They shouted until they were hoarse.
The noise was so great that only a few of them standing near
the cross heard what He said when His lips moved in prayer:

> "Father, forgive them, for they know not what they
> do."

One of the thieves, drugged and half-drunk, cried out to
Jesus:

> "Can't You see how we suffer?
> If You are the Son of God, take us down from these
> crosses. Save us and Yourself."

The thief cried for salvation—but only for salvation from nails and a cross—not for salvation from himself and the hell that his own deeds had wrought.

Then pain gripped him, and he began to curse and to swear, blaming Jesus for the pain.

But the other turned his head so that he could see Jesus, and he said to his companion:

> "Dost not thou fear God, seeing thou art in the same condemnation? And we indeed justly; for we receive the due reward of our deeds: but this man hath done nothing amiss."

Then he said to Jesus, "Remember me when Thou comest into Thy Kingdom."

And Jesus, His face drawn with suffering, but His voice still kind, answered:

> "This very day when this pain is over, we shall be together . . . thou and I . . . in Paradise."

And the man, comforted, set his lips to endure to the end.

The sun rose higher and higher.

Time oozed but slowly like the blood that dripped from the cross. . . .

Jesus opened His eyes again and saw His mother standing there with John beside her.

He called out the name of John, who came closer.

Strength was fast ebbing away; an economy of words was necessary. . . .

> "Thou wilt take care of her, John?" . . .

And John, choked with tears, put his arm 'round the shoulders of Mary.

Jesus said to His mother: "He will be thy son."
His lips were parched, and He spoke with difficulty.
He moved His head uneasily against the hard wood of the cross, as a sick man moves his head on a hot pillow.

The women beneath the cross stood praying for Jesus and for the thieves.
The centurion was silent, although every now and then he would look up at Jesus with a strange look on his face . . .
           puzzled . . . wondering . . . marveling. . . .

The rest of the soldiers had been playing knucklebones in the shadow of the crosses.
Agreeing that they did not want to tear Christ's tunic—or seamless robe—they had tossed for it.
The Man on the cross would not need it again. . . .

Then, in the awful words of Matthew:

           "And sitting down they watched Him there."

There before their eyes was being enacted the tremendous drama of the redemption of mankind . . .
And they only sat and watched.

They were unwitting actors in the supreme event of which the prophets had dreamed. . . .
They were witnesses, standing at the crossroads of history.
And they saw—*nothing!*

The sky was growing strangely dark.
A thunderstorm seemed to be blowing up from the mountains and clouds hid the sun.
Women on the converging highways beyond the hill took children by the hand and began hurrying back to the city.
People looked up at the sky and became frightened.
The darkening sun at noon caused bird songs to freeze in fear as their melodies trailed off in the gathering shadows.
It was an uncanny darkness.

The shouting died away.
Now even the soldiers were silent.
They put away their dice. Their gambling was done.
  They had won . . . and lost.

Suddenly, Jesus opened His eyes and gave a loud cry.
The gladness in His voice startled all who heard it.
For it sounded like a shout of victory:
> "It is finished! Father, into Thy hands
> I commit My spirit."

And with that cry He died.
It was the ninth hour. . . .

Yes, "He saved others; Himself He cannot save."
But they were wrong as well as right.
Could He not have saved Himself?

He might have followed the advice of His friends and avoided Jerusalem altogether at the feast time.

He might have left the garden that night instead of quietly
waiting there for Judas.
He might have compromised with the priests—and made a
bargain of future silence with Caiaphas.
Had not Pilate almost pleaded with Him for an excuse, any
excuse, for not sending Him to His death?

He might have made His Kingdom political instead of
spiritual.
    That would have pleased and silenced Judas.
He might have chosen the expedient.
As He Himself reminded Peter, He might have called upon
twelve legions of angels to rescue Him and to show His great
power.

Yes, He might have saved Himself.
He had the power; many ways of escape were available. . . .
    But then He would never have been our Savior!

Had not Christ said, "I am the good shepherd: the good
shepherd gives His life for the sheep"?
Gives His *life?* . . .

But could not our salvation have been consummated without
that final price?
No, for when men sin to the uttermost, when sin sinks to its
final degradation, no mere palliatives nor mild remedies can
deal with it.

What then?
In a world where death by crucifixion was still possible no

polite and perfumed half-measures could suffice.
A blood transfusion was necessary . . .
                            rich, red blood
                            human blood.
And if talk of blood offends us, let us remember that
crucifixion would offend us, too.

Perhaps we need to be reminded that our religion is not all
sweetness and light.

Christianity is much more than pretty pictures of Jesus
among flowers and singing birds, moving with a smile
among simple folk.
The Gospel is much more than the Golden Rule . . .
    much more than the Christmas story
       and the fair green hills of Galilee.

Christianity deals with reality,
    with life as you and I experience it.
For it recognizes that this is not always a pretty world.
It is a world in which dreadful things can happen.

The faith that is nourished and sustained by the Spirit of God
faces frankly these human situations that often make our
faith difficult.

More than that, Christianity has a cross at the very heart of
it.
Leave out Calvary, and Christianity dwindles to a weak and
empty cult—to a system of impossible ethics.

It would not be good news to preach that there was no sin in
Jesus Christ

therefore we ought to be like Him.
It is not good news to say that He did no wrong,
    therefore we too ought to be perfect.
It is not good news to say that He left us an example that we
should follow . . .
These things are true—but they are not a Gospel.
Christ did not come into the world merely to proclaim a new
morality
    or a code of ethics
        or to set up a new social order.
He did not show men how to work out their own salvation
by good deeds
    by charities
        or by trying to live respectable lives.

He came, He said, "to save that which was lost. . . ."
He came to save all those who were lost in the sense that
they had lost their way. . . .

> "How think ye? If a man have an hundred sheep,
> and one of them be gone astray, doth he not leave
> the ninety and nine, and goeth into the mountains,
> and seeketh that which is gone astray?"

Never was there in Him condemnation for the lost . . . only
the desire to help the lost one back to the path . . .
    back to right relations with His Father . . .
        back home again.

Yet He well knew our human willfulness.
He knew that after making allowances for heredity and
environment

for education
and example
and the tyranny of habit
there is still a central shrine of freedom in every life.

There is a place where *we* do it, and no one else—
where *we* are responsible for our own choices—
and we know it.

"All we like sheep have gone astray;
we have turned every one to his own way. . . ."

How would He deal with the iniquity
of our human willfulness? . . .

"And the Lord hath laid on Him the iniquity of us
all.

"Therefore I will divide Him a portion with the
great,
and He shall divide the spoil with the strong;
because He hath poured out His soul to death:
and He was numbered with the transgressors;
and He bare the sin of many, and made intercession
for the transgressors."

Then there were the sick. . . .
"They that be whole need not a physician," He had said,
"but they that are sick"—
the sinsick, the sick of mind, the sick of body.
And He who could not tolerate sickness or disease,
in whom there was a passion for health and wholeness,
must somehow deal with that, too.

How should He do it? . . .

> ". . . Upon Him was the chastisement that
> made us whole,
> and with His stripes we are healed. . . ."

And the last enemy, Death . . .
   that final fear lurking deep in every human heart . . .
That enemy, too, must be put down.

How should He do it?
Who but God could deal with all the sin of the ages . . .
      all the suffering of the flesh . . .
   all the sorrow of the heart?

None but God!

But not a God sitting on a gilded throne high up in the
heavens,
   not some ethereal, nebulous God floating about in space
   like a benevolent cloud . . .
   not some four- or five-dimensional deity created by a
   Greek philosopher . . .
But a God walking through your front door and mine . . .
A God who lives and feels and understands . . .
A God who can sympathize . . . who has explored the vast
treasuries of pain . . .
A God who knows what it feels like to weep . . .
A God who can remember the feeling of a tear trickling down
the cheek . . .

Someone utterly pure—in whom there is no spot
                                                   nor blemish
                                                   nor taint . . .

Someone willing to give Himself at whatever cost of pain and
suffering and death within this time process, and in the form
of the life that you and I know . . . taking shape—the body
of a man . . . the form of a servant . . .
  with a voice to speak to us . . .
    a heart to feel for us . . .
      eyes to weep with us . . .
      hands to bless and to be nailed to a cross.

> "Surely He has borne our griefs,
>   and carried our sorrows. . . .
> He was oppressed, and He was afflicted,
>   yet He opened not His mouth:
> like a lamb that is led to the slaughter,
> and like a sheep that before its shearers
>   is dumb,
> so He opened not His mouth.
> By oppression and judgment He was taken away;
> and as for His generation, who considered that He
> was cut off out of the land of the living, stricken for
> the transgression of my people?"

The Gospel message is simply that—that such a thing has
come to pass. . . .

This is the good news the Church has to proclaim . . .
that there is available for us today a Sin Doctor who will
come to you and to me and heal us, if we will but let Him
into our lives . . .
Whose gracious Spirit will mysteriously steal into our hearts
and show us the doorway to a new life. . . .

Thus the Gospel is not something to do—
      but something done.
The Gospel is not a demand—
      but a supply.
Not something you can do—
      but something that has been done for you.

And it happened at a certain point in time . . .
      on the brow of a hill shaped like a skull.
It was done for me—and for you—simply because He loves
us.

Had not Jesus said to His apostles that last memorable night
with them in the Upper Room . . .

      "Greater love hath no man than this, that a man lay
      down his life for his friends."

That is why a hideous cross has become the world's symbol
of blessing.

It was plain to be seen that the Nazarene was dead.
He had died after only six hours of suffering.
Long enough, surely . . .
Yet the Roman centurion who watched could not believe that
any crucified one could die in just six hours.
To make sure, one of the soldiers pierced Christ's side with
a spear, and the last remaining drops of His blood were
poured out.

Yes, He was dead . . .
There was no need to break His legs in an effort
to hasten the end.

During those last hours, John had tried over and over to
persuade Mary to leave—but she would not.
Her son was hanging there . . .

So long as there was a breath of life—no—she would
not leave Him.

But Mary herself was nearing a state of collapse.
When it was over, she flung herself on John's breast . . .

                                    sobbing . . . quietly.
Then John lifted her up, put his arms around her shoulders,
and gently led her down the hill toward home.
And Salome, John's own mother, who had been watching
afar off with some of the other women from the outskirts of
the crowd, seeing the little tableau, left the others and came
running to help.

"That one didn't take long," the soldiers said, as they
prepared to fall in line and march back to their barracks.

"Dead so soon?" inquired Pilate, when Joseph of Arimathea—a member of the Great Jewish Council—came to him
to ask for the body of Jesus.
According to Roman custom the body of an executed criminal
belonged to the relatives or friends, so that by his request
Joseph had now openly avowed his faith in the prophet.

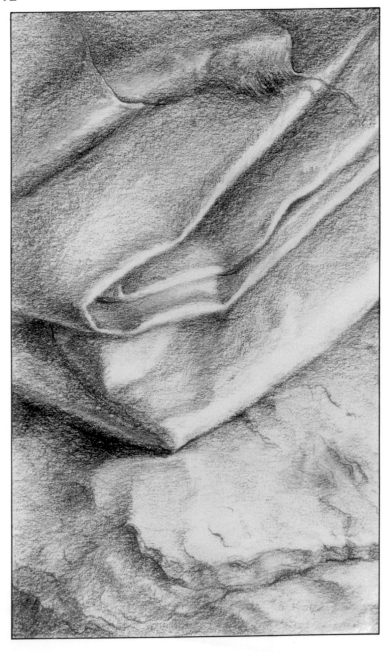

This request surprised Pilate, for the Councilor was a rich man and a distinguished one—not the usual type to acknowledge himself as a follower of the Nazarene.
Not until the centurion, having been summoned, confirmed the statement that the Galilean was really dead, did Pilate grant Joseph his request.

In some haste—lest anyone else should meddle in the matter—Joseph, with Nicodemus to help him, then took down the disfigured body from the cross.
Gently they wound it in strips of clean linen eight feet long with spices between the layers—as was the custom of the Jews.

And as their hands busied themselves with the sad work, words from the prophet Isaiah came winging their way into Joseph's mind.
He had learned them as a child in the synagogue . . .
had often recited them to the elders.
How strange that he should remember them at this moment . . .

 as if they had a special significance . . .
  as if—as if—they were meant for him. . . .
   ". . . And they made His grave with the wicked
    and with a rich man in His death,
   although He had done no violence,
    and there was no deceit in His mouth. . . ."

And Nicodemus was remembering, too, remembering that night when he had laid aside his work for the Sanhedrin, turned down the lamp, and gone out under the stars to ask questions of the Galilean. . . .

For all the rest of my life, he thought, *whenever the wind moans or tugs at my robes—I shall be remembering that musical voice:*

> "The wind bloweth where it listeth, and thou hearest the sound thereof, but canst not tell whence it cometh, and whither it goeth: so is every one that is born of the Spirit."

And now He was dead. . . .
Nicodemus was tortured by the knowledge of all the things he might have said while Jesus lived.
So many things he might have done. . . .

Now, he thought, *it is too late.*
And as he looked at the still face of his Friend, unashamedly he watched his tears making little smudges on the white linen.

Then Joseph and Nicodemus carried the body of their Lord to a newly made tomb in the Councilor's garden—a tomb which he had had hewn out of the rock for himself.

After the Sabbath they would arrange for a burial with proper ceremony.
All they could do at the moment was to make sure of a decent provisional burial without interference on the part of the priests.
It would be enough to roll a great round stone to the door of the sepulchre, for the evening star was already shining . . . and no more work could be done until the Sabbath was over.

The two men—and the women, Mary Magdalene, and Mary, the mother of Joses, who had followed at a distance to see where the body of their Master was being laid—went away very silent . . . very sad. . . .

On the morrow the Roman governor was told that a group of priests and Pharisees sought audience with him.
Pilate undoubtedly suspected that even yet he was not finished with the matter of the Nazarene—and he was right.

The priests remembered only too well Pilate's mood when they had asked that the inscription for Christ's cross be changed . . .
So they selected the most softspoken and diplomatic member of the group and thrust him forward as their spokesman:

> "Sire, we remember that Jesus, that deceiver, said while He was yet alive, 'After three days I will rise again.'

> "Command therefore, we pray you, that the sepulchre be made sure until the third day, lest His disciples come by night, and steal Him away, and say unto the people, He is risen from the dead: so the last error shall be worse than the first."

The priests irritated Pilate.
He thought of having washed his hands in the golden bowl such a few hours before . . . "I am innocent of the blood of this just person: see ye to it. . . ."
But somehow he had not been able to wash his hands of it.
The case kept coming back and back. . . .

He leaned forward in his gilded chair and wearily passed his hands across his eyes.

Then he almost roared at the priests:

> "No! I will not send a Roman guard. That's
> nonsense. . . . The man is dead. What care I what His
> disciples say? You have your own watch. Make it as
> sure as you can . . . Now—go your way."

And he waved his arm for the priests to be escorted from the
audience chamber.

So—in the ironic words of Matthew:

> ". . . They went, and made the sepulchre sure,
> sealing the stone, and setting a watch."

I t was still dark. . . .
Through the deserted streets of Jerusalem three men were
hurrying, almost running toward the residence of the high
priest.
In the courtyard a slave lifted a torch to see their faces. . . .
"See Caiaphas now? At this hour? Impossible . . .
You will have to wait until the dawn at least."

An hour-and-a-half later the three men reported to Caiaphas
that the tomb of the executed Nazarene—which they had
been sent to guard—was empty.
Caiaphas was at first puzzled, then angry, then thoughtful
. . . for the men had no explanation.
Repeated questioning could not shake their story.

No—they had not gone to sleep. . . .
There had been a strange stirring in the garden. . . .
They had thought they had heard something. . . .
Investigation had found the tomb empty—
That was all.

Caiaphas requested that the men tell their weird story again
later on that day to the elders meeting in plenary session. . . .

> "And when they were assembled with the elders,
> and had taken counsel, they gave large money unto
> the soldiers, saying, Say ye, His disciples came by
> night, and stole Him away while we slept.
>
> "And if this come to the governor's ears, we will
> persuade him, and secure you.
>
> "So they took the money, and did as they were
> taught. . . ."

Meanwhile the despair and disillusionment in Simon Peter's
heart were complete . . .
despair over the shamefulness of his own denial . . .
disillusionment over the fate of Jesus of Nazareth.
For Peter and the other apostles had hoped that this One
would redeem Israel.
Now all hope was gone: Christ was *dead* . . .
hailed as King on the Sabbath before . . .
dead like a common thief on Friday.

"I go fishing," Peter said to the others.
What else was there to do?

Life had to go on, be picked up where they had dropped it
when, at the imperious call of a Stranger, they had aban-
doned their fishing nets and left everything to follow Him.

Perhaps away from Jerusalem with its bitter memories, they
could forget.
Perhaps with the sea wind once again fanning
their cheeks . . .
      with the rough nets sliding through their fingers . . .
    with the feel of the tug of fish
they could forget a certain Face
  a Voice with music in it
    a Smile . . .
      Perhaps. . . .

The women, too, who had ministered to the little band of
apostles, were just as despairing—only, as women will, they
were trying to work out their grief in a different way.

They had watched from a distance as Joseph of Arimathea
and Nicodemus had hastily anointed the body of Jesus.
At the first possible moment they would complete the
anointing. . . .
So before light dawned on that Sunday morning Mary
Magdalene, Salome, the mother of James the Greater and of
John, and Mary were on their way to the tomb where Jesus'
body had been laid.

As they walked in the half-light, they were preoccupied with
one problem . . .

      "And they said among themselves, Who shall roll us
      away the stone from the door of the sepulchre?"

But even as they pondered . . .

> ". . . When they looked, they saw that the stone was
> rolled away: for it was very great. . . .
>
> "And they went out quickly, and fled
> from the sepulchre; for they trembled and
> were amazed. . . ."

What did it mean?
Someone had tampered with Jesus' tomb.
Perhaps His body had been stolen. . . .

But the women were so frightened that they did not wait to
investigate.
They had only fled. . . .
Mary Magdalene, being younger than the others, outran
them.
But ere she had reached the road, she met Simon Peter and
John—Simon had planned to pay his last respects before he
left for Galilee.
Breathlessly Mary blurted out:

> "They have taken away the Lord out of the sepul-
> chre, and we know not where they have laid
> him. . . ."

The two men were shocked; they too started running, but
John outran Peter.
And when they stooped down and saw what was in the
sepulchre, they believed.
Believed *what?*
Not, as Mary thought, that Jesus' body had been stolen—
But that Jesus of Nazareth was alive!

John and Peter, as they went into the grave in the garden that first Easter morning, did not know *what* to think—until they saw what was inside the grave—

> *And then they believed.*

The inside of the tomb revealed something that proved the Resurrection.
What was it?
Let us turn to the narrative again and read carefully:

> "Then cometh Simon Peter following him, and went into the sepulchre, and seeth the linen clothes lie, And the napkin, that was about his head, not lying with the linen clothes, but wrapped together in a place by itself. Then went in also that other disciple, which came first to the sepulchre, and he saw, and believed."

In this connection, it is well for us to remember that the stone was rolled away from the door, not to permit Christ to come out, but to enable the disciples to go in.

Notice what it was they saw.
They saw the linen clothes lying, not unwound and carefully folded, as some people appear to think—

> not thrown aside as is a covering when one rises from bed,
> but lying there on the stone slab in the shape of the body.

True, the napkin had been removed and folded, but the grave-clothes were lying there, mute but eloquent evidence that a living organism had come out.

The grave-clothes lay like the shriveled, cracked shell of a

cocoon, left behind when the moth has emerged and hoisted her bright sails in the sunshine . . .
Or, more accurately, like a glove from which the hand has been removed, the fingers of which still retain the shape of the hand.

In that manner, the grave-clothes were lying, collapsed a little, slightly deflated—because there was between the rolls of bandages a considerable weight of spices, but there lay the linen cloth that had been wound 'round the body of Christ.

It was when they saw *that*, that the disciples believed.

The Greek word here for "see"—*theōrei*—is not to behold as one looks at a spectacle, not to see as the watchmaker who peers through his magnifying glass.
It means to see with inner light that leads one to conclusion.

It is perception
   reflection
      understanding—more than sight.
Do you *see?*

It is to see, as one who reasons from the effect to the cause.
And when John and Peter reasoned from what they saw in the tomb, they arrived at the conclusion
     the unshakable
    unassailable
   certain conviction
that Jesus Christ had risen from the dead.

 But Mary Magdalene, still weeping, lingered at the edge of the garden.

Along with the other women, she had come to find a dead body . . . and had been shocked to find the grave empty. She thought it had been broken open—grave-robbers, perhaps.
She did not know . . .
She could not think clearly.
Only one thought seems to have absorbed her soul—
the body of the Lord had been lost . . . she must find Him!

She ran as never before back toward the empty tomb, with the speed and unawareness of time and distance that grief or fear or love can impart. . . .

> "But Mary stood without at the sepulchre weeping: and as she wept, she stooped down, and looked into the sepulchre . . . She turned herself back, and saw Jesus standing, and knew not that it was Jesus.

> "Jesus saith unto her, Woman, why weepest thou? whom seekest thou?"

And John tells us that she thought He was the gardener. She fell at His feet, her eyes brimming with tears—her head down—sobbing, "Sir, if thou hast taken Him hence, tell me where thou hast laid Him, and I will take Him away."

To her tortured mind there was a gleam of hope that perhaps the gardener, for some reason known only to him, had moved the body . . .
She was red-eyed . . .
She had not slept since Friday . . .
There had been no taste for food . . .

She had been living on grief and bereaved love. . . .

     "Jesus saith unto her, Mary."

His voice startled her . . .
She would have recognized it anywhere.
She lifted her head with a jerk . . . blinked back the tears
from her eyes and looked—right into His eyes.

She knew . . . her heart told her first and then her mind . . .
She saw the livid marks of the nails in His hands and looking
up into His face, she whispered:
     "Rabboni!"

The loveliest music of that first Easter dawn is the sound of
those words echoing in the garden . . .
   His gentle . . . "Mary"
     and her breathless . . . "Master!"

Mary had come prepared to weep—
   Now she could worship.
She had come expecting to see Him lying in the tomb—
   She had found Him walking in the newness of resurrected
   life.

So much had happened in those last few days.
To Cleopas and his friend, the week that had closed seemed
like a terrible dream.

Event had followed event in a swiftness that had left no time for meditation.
As the two men walked along the winding road to Emmaus, it was of these things they spoke.

There had been Christ's entry in triumph into the holy city. To all of them, it had seemed that—at last—their Messiah would enter into His own.
Surely, the days of Roman occupation would now soon be over. Exactly when the Messiah would announce Himself and declare their independence, they did not know.

Joyously, the multitudes thronged around Him, awaiting the good news.

Then, swiftly, there had been woven around the Nazarene a net of intrigue—soon to be drawn tighter and tighter.

There had been that night when Judas had turned on his heel and left the Upper Room to keep his treacherous rendezvous.
There had been Jesus' strange words of dismissal, as He had watched Judas disappear into the night.

Then the scene that followed in the garden
out on the hillside . . .
Would they ever forget it?

In the silence of the night, Jesus prostrate in prayer . . .
          the bright Syrian stars seeming to fill the sky . . .
          the gnarled olive trees casting grotesque shadows . . .
          a swinging lantern coming up the winding path . . .

the rabble of Temple doorkeepers and Temple police, who had laid aside their brooms and their keys long enough to come out with Judas to arrest the Galilean . . .
How could they ever forget?

As Cleopas and his companion talked,
they became more and more engrossed.
Their words came pouring out in a torrent of recollection.

There had been the despicable kiss of Judas . . .
    the arrest itself . . .
        the foolhardiness of Peter with his little sword . . .
            the return to the city . . .
                Peter's blasphemous denial by the fire . . .
                    the all-night vigil.

The rest was an agony of painful memories . . .
    the scourging of Christ in front of Pilate's palace . . .
        the bloodthirsty cries of the mob . . .
            the march to Golgotha . . .
                those awful moments
    when the sound of a hammer had echoed across the valley.

There had been the ravings and curses of the thieves on their crosses . . .
    the strange, eerie darkness . . . and the earthquake . . .
And the death of Him whom they had learned to love, of Him whom they had called . . . "Master."

So engrossed were the two men in these memories, that they

did not notice the approach of a Stranger.
Suddenly, there He was walking beside them.

And He said to them, "What is this conversation which you
are holding with each other as you walk?"

And they stood still, looking sad.
Then one of them, Cleopas, answered him,
   "Are you the only visitor to Jerusalem who does not know
the things that have happened there in these days?"
And He said to them, "What things?"

And they said to Him, "Concerning Jesus of Nazareth, who
was a prophet mighty in deed and word before God and all
the people, and how our chief priests and rulers delivered
Him up to be condemned to death and crucified Him.
But we had hoped that He was the one to redeem Israel.
Yes, and besides this, it is now the third day
since this happened.

"Moreover, some women of our company amazed us.
They were at the tomb early in the morning and did not find
His body; and they came back saying . . . He was alive. . . ."

And He said to them, "O foolish men, and slow of heart to
believe all that the prophets have spoken!
Was it not necessary that the Christ should suffer these
things and enter into His glory?"

And He began with Moses and all the prophets and ex-
plained to them all the Scriptures that referred to Himself.

Thus did the walk of seven-and-a-half miles pass quickly. And when they reached Emmaus, the sun was fast sinking behind the copper hills.

The shadows were long . . . soon it would be dark.

The two men begged the mysterious Stranger to spend the night with them, or at least to share their evening meal.
Still they did not know who He was.
Why?
Largely because Christ was the last person these disciples expected to see.
Had they not seen Him die?
Had they not watched His head fall limp on His shoulders?

It had seemed so absurd to them as they had stood at the foot of the cross and remembered His words:

> "Whosoever believeth in Me, though he were dead, yet shall he live . . . and whosoever liveth and believeth in Me shall never die . . ."

Then to see Him die—right there before their eyes. . . .

They had not been able to grasp the glorious truth that life hereafter is not dependent upon the physical at all . . . is not material but spiritual.
So the disciples imagined that Jesus of Nazareth could not possibly be alive unless He were just as He was before . . .
dependent upon the same material limitations that bounded their lives.

And so they sat down at last to eat their evening meal.
The Stranger stayed with them and, in the most natural way
in the world, gave thanks before He took bread in His hands.

There was something in the way He gave thanks . . .
   as He took bread . . .
      reached across the table . . .
         broke the bread with characteristic gesture . . .
           and the folds of His robe fell back . . .
Perhaps they saw the livid red marks of the nails in His
hand.
But whatever it was, in that instant they knew . . .
They knew!
And He was gone.

It wasn't possible!
It couldn't be . . .
But they had seen Him with their own eyes.
Then the women were right!
And they rose and ran—ran, not walked,
all the seven-and-a-half miles back to Jerusalem to tell the
other disciples the incredible news.

But they found some of the disciples completely unwilling to
believe what they were reporting.
Salome and Mary, the mother of James the Less and of Joses,
had been there much earlier in the day and had already told
them the news of the empty tomb.
Then Mary Magdalene had appeared—her eyes shining like
stars—saying . . .
     "I have seen the Lord!"

But these women were emotional creatures.
How could their testimony be accepted as credible?

> "And their words seemed to them as idle tales, and
> they believed them not."

Then Peter and John had appeared not only talking about the
empty tomb, but offering an explanation for it—
an explanation they could not, would not accept.
Resurrection? Impossible!
How could intelligent men believe *that?*

And now the breathless Cleopas and his friend with the
same words that Mary Magdelene had used . . .

> "We have seen the Lord!"

Seen a dead man? Impossible!
Had everyone suddenly gone crazy?

Thomas, one of the disciples, thrust out his jaw and stepped
forward.
He said what some of the others had been wanting to say
. . .

> "I don't believe you. . . . What we've all been
> through must have temporarily unhinged your
> minds. . . . I would have to see the Lord for myself.
> Not only that, except I shall see in His hands the
> print of the nails, and put my finger into the print of
> the nails, and thrust my hand into His side,
> *I will not believe."*

It was eight days before Thomas got his proof.

Once again the disciples were gathered together,
Thomas among them.
Suddenly Jesus was with them in the room.
He singled Thomas out, smiled at him:

> "Reach hither thy finger, and behold My hands; and
> reach hither thy hand, and thrust it into My side;
> and be not faithless, but believing."

Thomas was all but overwhelmed.
Gone was all his blustering skepticism.
He fell to his knees . . . All he could say was . . .

> "My Lord and my God."

Simon Peter witnessed this.
There was now no doubt in his heart . . .
Something tremendous had indeed happened.
The Christ who had been crucified was alive . . .
Life could never be the same again!

Yet something else troubled Simon, ate at him.
He was still nursing deep and bitter shame, still smarting
with the searing iron that had eaten into his very soul.

He had denied his Lord.
How could he ever face Him again?

Whenever Simon was deeply troubled, always he went back
to his nets.
"I go a-fishing," he would say . . . and this time six of his
friends decided to go with him.

There came the night when the men had worked hard and had caught nothing.

As they rowed back toward shore, discouraged and in comparative silence, they saw Someone standing on the beach in the early light of morning. The sea was calm—calm as a millpond—and a light early-morning mist still clung to the surface of the water.

"Children, have ye any meat?"

And when they replied in the negative, the voice called:

"Cast the net on the right side of the ship,
and ye shall find."

They had nothing to lose in following the Stranger's advice. Over the side went the nets again, this time with success— so much success that the nets were in danger of breaking.

They were now getting closer to the shore, and the mist was beginning to lift.

They could see flames leaping from a fire on the beach, and this mysterious Figure waiting for them to beach their boat.

"It is the Lord," said John, and that was enough for Simon. Here was the opportunity for which he had longed—to tell the Lord that he loved Him—to show how well he knew Him.

Without a moment's hesitation, he jumped overboard and waded ashore.

And then comes the loveliest record of God dealing with a penitent sinner. . . .

Its tenderness and understanding come stealing into our own hearts like the perfume of crushed flowers.

As they sat 'round the fire, cooking some of the fish they had caught and baking their loaves of bread on the live coals, Jesus suddenly turned to Simon. . . .

"Simon, son of Jonas, lovest thou Me
more than these?"

Simon was a little puzzled at the question:

"Yes, Lord, Thou knowest that I love Thee."

Christ looked him straight in the eyes. . . .

"Then—feed My lambs."

Then again He asked:

"Simon, son of Jonas, lovest thou Me?"

Simon was a little hurt. Why would the Lord *keep* asking?

"Yes, Lord, Thou knowest that I love Thee."
"Then—feed My sheep."

But when the question came the third time, light began to dawn for Simon.
For every one of Simon's earlier denials Jesus was now asking a pledge of love.
This was His way of making everything all right again.

When next we see Simon, he is Simon no more—
but Peter—the Rock.

We see him fearless and eloquent,
  fire in his eyes
    and his voice vibrant with conviction,
    melodious with good news.

His own will has gone; his Master's will has taken its place.
Peter stands up and preaches the Gospel of his crucified and
risen Lord.

Furthermore he is preaching it in Jerusalem, at the storm-
center of the enemies of the Nazarene.

Implicit in the whole situation is the fact that on the day of
the crucifixion the disciples did not ever expect to see Christ
again.
The Resurrection was the last thing they expected.
Their belief in it was not some fantastic idea, wafted in from
the swamps of fevered imaginations.
It was not some romantic wish out of their dream-house, not
the result of wishful thinking.
For it had come as a complete shock,
  unexpected
    bewildering.

There is no more adamant fact in the records than the
changes that came over these men.
Jerusalem had been anything but impressed with the way
Christ's disciples had conducted themselves during the
arrest and trial of the Nazarene.
His followers had certainly not been courageous.
In fact, they had all either fled to save their own lives or
followed at a great distance.

Peter was so fearful that he had even denied having known
the Nazarene.

Then after their Master's death, the band of disciples had
stayed in hiding with the doors locked—"for the fear of the
Jews."

Yet after that first Easter morning, we find these same men
   timid
      frightened
         ineffective
preaching openly, with no fear of anyone.

Their personal conviction rings like a bell through the pages
of the New Testament . . . steady and strong. . . .

> "That which we have heard with our own ears,
> seen with our own eyes, handled with
> our own hands, declare we unto you."

And of what were they so sure?
That Jesus Christ was alive—but no spiritual resurrection
this—not just the perpetuation of a dead man's ideas.

No, by a Resurrection they meant that suddenly, at a given
time in that new tomb that had belonged to Joseph of
Arimathea, there had been a fluttering of unseen forces . . .
   a rustling as of the breath of God moving through the
   garden.

Strong, immeasurable life had been breathed back into the
dead body they had laid upon the cold stone slab;

And the dead man had risen up
> had come out of the grave-clothes
> had walked to the threshold of the tomb
> had stood swaying for a moment on His wounded feet
and had walked out into the dewy garden alive forevermore.

It was so real to them that they could have almost heard the
whispered sigh as the spirit had fluttered back into the worn
body . . .
Almost catch a whiff of the strange scents that had drifted
back to Him from the tomb
> of linen and bandages . . .
>> of spices—myrrh and aloes . . .
>>> and close air and blood.

Furthermore, they were saying these things in the same city
that had sought to destroy the Christ,
> right at the door of the stronghold of the priests,
>> a thousand paces from the tomb where Christ had been
>> laid.

Christ's enemies would have given anything to have refuted
their claims.
One thing would have done it—so simply.
If only they could have produced a body.
But they could not. . . .

So they tried everything else they could think of to silence
these fishermen, tax collectors, farmers, carpenters, shep-
herds, housewives . . .
> imprisonment

threats
   scourgings
      stonings and death.
Nothing succeeded in silencing them.

There would come the time when Peter would actually stand before Caiaphas and the Sanhedrin, as Jesus had done, and nothing but flaming words of courage would pass his lips:

> "Whether it be right in the sight of God to hearken unto you more than unto God, judge ye.
> For we cannot but speak the things which we have seen and heard. . . ."

Now it takes a very great conviction to change men so drastically.
Nor do men persist in a lie or even a delusion, if every time they insist on its truth, they are driving nails into their own coffins.

Men do not invent a story, so that they can be crucified upside-down, as Peter eventually was . . .
  or have their heads chopped off, like Paul, outside the city of Rome,
      or be stoned to death—like Stephen.

A self-hypnotic illusion may sustain men for a time—
but not for long.
In the long run, an illusion does not build character strong enough to stand great hardship, great persecution.
Only the bedrock truth can do that!

Moreover, men who are merely fooling themselves do not become purposeful men

well-integrated men with self-sustaining qualities of leadership . . .
as these erstwhile timid apostles became.

And here is something else—it was their continuing fellowship with their risen Lord through the years that became the integrating
  guiding
    sustaining
power in their lives.

Through His Spirit they had guidance and strength. . . .
They had His wisdom.
  His peace
    and His joy.
They had boldness and courage and they had power . . .
  qualities that they had not had until after the first Easter
  morning.

They now felt that they were still in touch with Him . . .
  in a different way—yes—but in a more powerful way.
The knew that He was still with them, even as He had promised. . . .

      "Go ye into the world and lo, I am with you
      always."

They felt that! They knew it!
The promises He had made to them before His death were now fulfilled, and they (men like Cleopas and his friend) went up and down in the land. . . .
They crossed the sea.

They shook the Roman Empire until it tottered and fell.
They changed the world.

This is the fact we in this twentieth century cannot ignore.

Through the nineteen centuries that have followed in every
land there have been men and women who have experienced
the same fellowship . . .
   who have felt the same power in their lives . . .
     who have had the same peace and inner serenity . . .
       who have had the same joy and the
       same radiant victory.

They were not crackpots, morons, or lunatics.
Included among them were some of the greatest minds the
world has ever seen . . .

Some of the most brilliant thinkers
                philosophers
              scientists
           and scholars. . . .
They were not frustrated personalities who fled the world of
reality and found refuge in the dugouts of their own wistful
escapes from life.

On the contrary, most of them have been radiant souls filled
with an abiding joy, living to the full every golden hour, and
tasting the deepest joys of life.

Dismiss, as you will, the sentimentality, the hysteria and the
wishful thinking that may be born in times of crisis and

danger; there is still a residue of hard, stubborn testimony from men and women who have met Him.

And you, too, may have that fellowship with the risen Christ.
Indeed, you will not believe the fact of the Resurrection for yourself until the living Christ lives in your own heart.
When you have in your own life that sense of His nearness and His power—ah, then, you too will *know!*

Your life today may be guided by Christ . . .
Your problems may be solved by His wisdom . . .
Your weakness may be turned into strength by His help . . .
Your struggles may become victories by His grace . . .
Your sorrows may be turned into joy by His comfort.

To you there may come the same wonderful changes that have come to other men and women all down through the years.

This is the reality that can be yours—this comradeship with the resurrected Christ through His Spirit is available now
. . .
  To the man in the street . . .
    to the government clerk . . .
      to the anxious mother . . .
        to the confused schoolboy or girl.

This is the real meaning of Easter.
Forget the bunny rabbits and the colored eggs.
Forget the symbols of spring that so often confuse and conceal the real meaning of what we celebrate on that day.

No tabloid will ever print the startling news that the mummified body of Jesus of Nazareth has been discovered in old Jerusalem.

Christians have no carefully embalmed body enclosed in a glass case to worship.

Thank God, we have an empty tomb.

The glorious fact that the empty tomb proclaims to us is that life for us does not stop when death comes.

Death is not a wall, but a door.

And eternal life which may be ours now, by faith in Christ, is not interrupted when the soul leaves the body,

for we live on . . . and on.

There is no death to those who have entered into fellowship with Him who emerged from the tomb.

Because the Resurrection is true, it is the most significant thing in our world today.

Bringing the resurrected Christ into our lives, individual and national, is the only hope we have for making a better world.

"Because I live, ye shall live also."

That is the message of Easter.

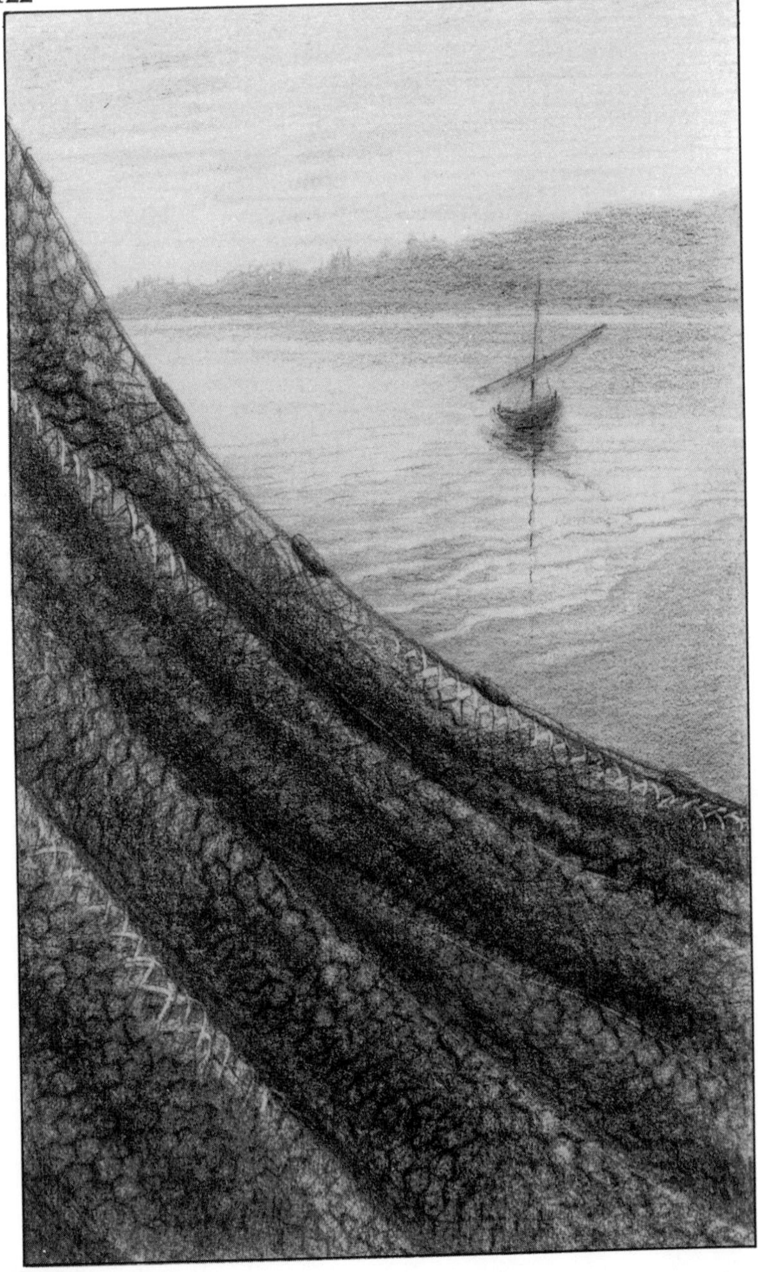